World-Class Fundraising Isn't a Solo Sport

OTHER BOOKS BY JEFFREY L. BULLER

A Toolkit for College Professors (with Robert E. Cipriano)
A Toolkit for Department Chairs (with Robert E. Cipriano)
Building Leadership Capacity: A Guide to Best Practices (with Walter H. Gmelch)
Change Leadership in Higher Education: A Practical Guide to Academic Transformation
Positive Academic Leadership: How to Stop Putting Out Fires and Start Making a Difference
Best Practices in Faculty Evaluation: A Practical Guide for Academic Leaders
Academic Leadership Day By Day: Small Steps That Lead to Great Success
The Essential Department Chair: A Comprehensive Desk Reference, Second Edition
The Essential Academic Dean: A Comprehensive Desk Reference, Second Edition
The Essential College Professor: A Practical Guide to an Academic Career

World-Class Fundraising Isn't a Solo Sport

The Team Approach to Academic Fundraising

Jeffrey L. Buller and Dianne M. Reeves

ROWMAN & LITTLEFIELD
Lanham • Boulder • New York • London

Published by Rowman & Littlefield
A wholly owned subsidiary of The Rowman & Littlefield Publishing Group, Inc.
4501 Forbes Boulevard, Suite 200, Lanham, Maryland 20706
www.rowman.com

Unit A, Whitacre Mews, 26-34 Stannary Street, London SE11 4AB

British Library Cataloguing in Publication Information Available

Library of Congress Cataloging-in-Publication Data Available

ISBN 978-1-4758-3158-0 (cloth : alk. paper)
ISBN 978-1-4758-3159-7 (pbk. : alk. paper)
ISBN 978-1-4758-3160-3 (electronic)

♾™ The paper used in this publication meets the minimum requirements of American National Standard for Information Sciences—Permanence of Paper for Printed Library Materials, ANSI/NISO Z39.48-1992.

Printed in the United States of America

Dedication

To all the colleagues whose talent and ideas inspired us in our work with donors, prospective donors, friends, and members of the community. There are many of you who came to mind as we faced different challenges and opportunities, asking ourselves "What would so-and-so do in this situation?" or "How might this person have handled it differently?" You have been our teachers, mentors, and role models, and we are grateful.

Table of Contents

Preface

Academic fundraising has always been a team effort. But, if you've been involved in the development work at colleges, universities, or community colleges for any time at all, you know that there's a world of difference between sending in a team to take advantage of a new opportunity and sending in your A Team. As we'll see in Chapter 1, your A Team consists of your top performers, the ones who set the standard for everyone else.

Everyone wants to have an A Team or become a member of one, but relatively few people know how to do so. We created this book to fill this need and explain some key strategies for developing the most effective team approach possible, basing it both on our own experiences and on our observations of other A Teams at institutions throughout the United States.

Although there are a lot of resources available to fundraising professionals and to academic leaders who are interested in fundraising, very few works address both sides of the institution simultaneously. That's a significant oversight since the most productive approach to institutional advancement is to partner academic administrators with development officers (DO) in a way that takes full advantage of the strengths of both.

As the higher education environment and the tax system that governs not-for-profit foundations become more and more complex, a team approach is almost essential. And if you're going to send in a team to take on your biggest fundraising challenges, why not send in your *best* team—your A Team?

We've written this book for academic leaders and DOs, those who are already experienced in fundraising but want to improve their skills and those who are just starting out and want to discover current best practices to use in their own advancement work. Courses, workshops, and seminars in academic fundraising might want to adopt *World-Class Fundraising Isn't a Solo Sport* as a guide or textbook. Presidents and provosts might consider giving a copy to every new dean, director, and department chair on their staff. And vice presidents (VPs) for advancement or community engagement might encourage the entire development staff to read it as a way of understanding the perspective of academic leaders, a point of view that is sometimes significantly different from their own.

Like its companion volume *Going for the Gold, World-Class Fundraising Isn't a Solo Sport* shares a number of stories that are adapted from the "real world" and that highlight experiences we've had working with academic administrators, DOs, and prospects or donors. Those incidents that we describe as witnessing ourselves always have a solid core of truth, but we've found it necessary to change certain details to protect the identities of those involved.

In other cases, incidents have been conflated for the sake of concision. For this reason, although the external details of a story may have been changed somewhat, the basic plotlines all relate to incidents we were involved in ourselves or saw unfold at our institutions. (We're embarrassed to admit that some of the people who made the mistakes in these case studies actually were us.) Regardless of whether the case study is intended to provide a positive or a negative example, our goal is always to illustrate ways in which you can improve the level of collaboration between the academic and development sectors of your school and demonstrate greater effectiveness, productivity, efficiency, and adherence to the highest ethical standards.

Each chapter concludes with a list of *references* (works cited in the chapter) and *resources* (works that haven't explicitly been cited but that can provide further information about the topics covered in that chapter). Four appendices at the end of the book offer additional material that any member of an A Team will find useful.

Both authors have numerous people to thank for their contributions to this book. Noteworthy among this group of generous colleagues are Sandy Ogden for her editorial insights, Ayn Patrick who helped with data input, Selene Vazquez who provided research support, and Magna Publications for allowing us to adapt and reuse some material in Chapter 2 that originally appeared in *Academic Leader*. (Reprint permission was granted by Magna Publications and *Academic Leader*.)

Jeffrey L. Buller and Dianne M. Reeves
Jupiter, Florida
May 15, 2016

Chapter One

Meet the A Team

If you want to travel fast, travel alone. If you want to travel far, travel together.

—*African Proverb*

Imagine this scenario: A university fundraiser is meeting with a prospective donor about possible support for a new arts center. The fundraiser is well prepared with answers to anything the prospect might ask about the center's cost, design, and potential use. But midway through the meeting, the discussion takes a sudden left turn. The potential donor asks whether the joint programming planned for the center will be multidisciplinary, cross-disciplinary, or interdisciplinary.

The fundraiser had always thought that those terms were synonyms and so tries to deflect this line of discussion by saying, "That's a very interesting question. I'll have to get back to you on that." But the potential donor keeps probing, with each question about academic programs becoming more explicit and (to the fundraiser) less comprehensible. It soon becomes clear that this conversation is moving in a very uncomfortable direction.

Or imagine this scenario: A dean is having lunch with a long-time supporter and hopes to secure a commitment to a new scholarship fund. The dean knows the supporter's interests well and has carefully tailored the discussion to resonate with issues this person cares deeply about. But as in the previous scenario, the discussion suddenly moves in an unexpected direction. The supporter asks, "What would be the best way for me to help with this? With a lead trust or a remainder trust? And if I make the commitment today, when will the gift be booked?"

The dean tries to move away from these topics by saying, "Those are questions that are probably best handled by our staff in legal affairs and the development office. But what I *can* tell you is ..." The prospective donor interrupts and proceeds to ask an increasing specific set of questions about gift agreements, tax implications, and ways of designating how the gift is to be used. It soon becomes clear that this conversation, too, is moving in a very uncomfortable direction.

It's time to send in the A Team.

What's an A Team? An A Team is a partnership of representatives from the academic side of the university, the office of development, and possibly other areas (such as legal affairs, human resources, and the office of grants and sponsored programs) who together have the knowledge and skills necessary to make a successful proposal for a significant gift, negotiate the terms of that gift, and speak authoritatively on behalf of the institution.

As such, individual members of the A Team have to know about fundraising policies, academic disciplines, legal requirements, institutional priorities, and a host of other issues. In addition to their knowledge, however, the members of the A Team have to be empowered to make certain decisions on their own. While major institutional commitments will, of course, require review at other levels of the college or university, the A Team should be endowed with sufficient autonomy that they can act officially in the name of the institution within a specified range of authority.

The core of an A Team will consist of two people: an *academic officer* (AO) who represents the teaching and research missions of the institution and a *development officer* (DO) who is a professional and highly trained fundraiser. The AO will usually have a title like provost, dean, or department chair (although for very large gifts this person's title may be president or chancellor), while the DO will often be the vice president (VP) for development, one of the VP's assistants or associates, director of development, development coordinator, or something similar.

Ancillary members of the A Team could be anyone whose knowledge and skills would potentially be valuable with respect to the gift being sought. They might be additional academic or development personnel, such as faculty members in specific disciplines, planned giving specialists, or other professionals who understand the implication of a gift in terms of its legal aspects, staffing requirements, impact on public relations, involvement of alumni, effect on student recruitment and enrollment management, and other relevant factors.

Due to the complexity of many institutional development efforts today, an extended A Team might even include marketing professionals who can help the others best promote and publicize their efforts to the community (see McAlexander, Koenig, and DuFault, 2014).

THE A TEAM CONCEPT

When most people use the expression A Team, they're referring to an organization's most elite and successful group of operatives. Highly skilled as individuals, each member of the A Team perfectly balances all other members so that the group as a whole works together with precision, efficiency, and impressive standards of achievement. Some A Teams are simply "born": They arise spontaneously out of a set of colleagues who are fortunate enough to match one another in skill while complementing one another in their areas of expertise. More frequently, however, A Teams are "made": They are created by bringing together a group of people who make a conscious effort to improve their skills in working together for greater success. It's this latter type of A Team that we're most interested in throughout this book. The A Teams that arise naturally don't require any advice from us. They're doing just fine on their own. But for those that may need a little help, there are specific strategies that can be applied to achieve greater results.

For academic fundraising, an A Team will be characterized by its

- Ability not just to meet but also to exceed its goals.
- Seemingly effortless mode of communication, with the result that all members of the group are clearly "on the same page" at all times.
- Camaraderie and strong support for one another.
- Willingness to let others shine for the good of the entire program.

In short, an A Team excels while others merely perform. An A Team "clicks," while others merely cooperate. And an A Team raises the bar, while others merely clear it.

The three most important areas in which an A Team is different from a group of colleagues who simply work together are the following:

- *Degree of communication.* An A Team operates in that "sweet spot" in which candor coexists with collegiality and where tacit cues are understood as completely as if they were spoken or written.
- *Breadth of knowledge.* An A Team comes as close as humanly possible to providing "one stop shopping" for academic fundraising. The knowledge and skills of its members are so diverse that it can answer nearly any question that might arise and solve nearly any problem that might be encountered.
- *Level of accomplishment.* An A Team doesn't just "talk the talk"; it also "walks the walk." Its achievements justify its reputation. It can always be counted on to get the job done, often ahead of schedule and with a higher level of success than was initially believed possible.

In the area of fundraising, your A Team will be the group that sets the example for others. It's the team that earns an A+ every single time, no matter how challenging the "test" or how intimidating the situation.

Of course, there's another reason why the expression A Team is appropriate for the topics we'll be addressing in this book. Its heart is a group of professionals from *A*cademic *A*ffairs and *A*dvancement (AAA) who meld perfectly to form a single cross-functional unit. (Notice that we're using the term *cross*-functional, not *dys*functional. There are far too many of those units in higher education as it is.) If you prefer, you can think of this group as your AAA Team.

But we rather like the symbolism that comes from melding all three As into a single letter. It represents how seamlessly Advancement and Academics can work together. As a result, if you're already a member of an A Team—or if you'd like to become one—you've come to exactly the right place. In the pages that follow, we'll explain how you can take an ordinary group of co-workers and gradually transform them into something extraordinary.

WHY A TEAM APPROACH TO FUNDRAISING IS NECESSARY

With your busy workload, why would you spend the time putting together an A Team when it would be much faster to do fundraising by yourself? Isn't it risky to bring along someone whose priorities might be different from yours and who might view building a new facility or endowing a scholarship fund as more important than the priorities you need to pursue?

Well, we could speak in platitudes about our work in higher education being larger than any one of us or the importance of collaboration in a system of shared governance, but the truth of the matter boils down to this: *When it comes to success in fund raising, you need to work as a team.* For one thing, complex projects require a knowledge base that no one person is likely to have. Anyone might be able to secure a few hundred dollars as a contribution to an annual fund. But when you want a gift that can utterly transform a program or an institution, it's best not to go it alone.

Of course, in order for a group to function at the level of an A Team, the members must all share the same understanding of the goal, focus, and rationale of what they're trying to do. The most effective way to achieve this goal is to create what is called a *development cascade*: a structure in which each component of a unit's fundraising goals flows organically from the mission of the institution (see Figure 1.1.).

In a well-designed development cascade, the institution's fundamental mission (outlining what the institution is now and why that role is important)

Mission Statement

Vision Statement

Stategic Plan

Tactical Plan

Fundraising Plan

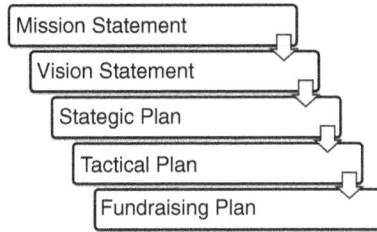

Figure 1.1. An Institution-Wide Development Cascade.

should inform its vision (what the institution intends to be in the future), which should in turn guide its strategy (how the institution will fulfill that vision), which should shape its tactics (what the institution is doing right now in order to implement that strategy), which should guide its funding goals (how the institution will pay for the strategy and tactics that will allow it to fulfill its vision).

Just as a single all-encompassing development cascade connects the mission of the institution to its funding goals, so should there also be related cascades that tie the mission to the funding goals of each academic unit (see Figure 1.2.). In other words, for each individual discipline, the institution's mission guides its vision, which shapes the funding priorities for the division of academic affairs, which inform the goals of each college, which in turn help determine the goals of each department.

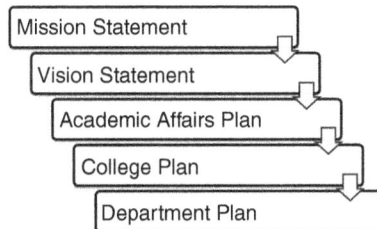

Mission Statement

Vision Statement

Academic Affairs Plan

College Plan

Department Plan

Figure 1.2. A Unit-Specific Development Cascade.

One of the characteristic features of an A Team is that every member understands precisely how that process works. A primary factor in an A Team's success is that the provost strongly supports what the deans are doing because their fundraising efforts advance his or her own goals, and the dean strongly supports what the chairs are doing for the same reason. It's the strategy known as *leading upwards*, and it's a practice commonly followed by effective administrators (see Buller, 2013, 183–186).

One of the most destructive ways in which fundraising practices can go awry occurs when individual units ignore the mission and plans of the administrative levels above it and dive immediately into a fundraising project—or worse, a mini-capital campaign—for a goal that dilutes the mission of the college or university. That type of dilution occurs because the gifts, as large as they may be, sometimes require additional resources to be redirected from a high institutional priority to this new, less significant purpose.

Even more frequently these "loose cannon fundraising efforts" waste people's time and alienate donors. After all, benefactors want to know how their gifts fit into the big picture of where the college or university is heading and why the institution wants to move in that particular direction. It's hard to provide those answers when you've begun your fundraising without giving careful attention to who you are, where you want to go, and how you intend to get there. A good rule of thumb, therefore, is that a development cascade should be completely redone every ten years or after a new chief executive officer has been hired, whichever comes first.

In both the development cascades represented by Figures 1.1 and 1.2, each level results in a tangible product, a guide that can be used on lower levels of the cascade. These resulting documents—ranging from the mission and vision statements of the entire institution to the fundraising plan of each concentration within a department—should adhere to what we call the *Three Ds*. In other words, they should be

- *Distinctive.* What is it that makes this program, college, or university different from others? What would the world lose if the institution or discipline didn't exist? What are its finest qualities?
- *Distilled.* How can this message be conveyed in the clearest, most concise manner? How can these ideas be expressed in a way that makes them immediately understandable by all the institution's stakeholders?
- *Directive.* How will the document produced at this level inform the college, university, or unit about what it should be *doing*? How can the statement be used to set priorities or make decisions among competing goals?

The sad fact is that many, if not most development cascades fail to meet even one of these three requirements. If you removed the name of a school from its mission and vision statements, put those statements in a pile with others that have been similarly redacted, and asked people to name the school that developed each one, very few institutions would be recognizable from what they say about their purpose and goals. (For an exercise of this sort, see Buller, 2015, 116–119.)

And yet these are the very documents that are supposed to guide that institution towards its future. Moreover, the goals that do become part of many strategic plans seem to have no other purpose than *mission creep*: the desire of every community college to be a state college, every state college to be a state university, every state university to be a research university, and every research university to be a research university with very high research activity (the category that used to be "Research I" universities in the old Carnegie system of classification).

In fact, becoming one of the Top Ten or Top Hundred Universities that [FILL IN THE BLANK] has become such a common objective that, if it could be achieved, there would have to be well more than a hundred schools on every top ten list and far more than a thousand among the top one hundred.

What A Teams do that others in development too often overlook is begin by reflecting on what the school does particularly well and why that's important for the school's service area. Growth can be a wonderful thing, but it shouldn't be the *only* measure of progress.

Rather than establish a vision about simply getting *bigger*, A Teams tend to focus on how the school and its academic programs intend to get *better*. In what ways have they historically transformed students' lives, perhaps bringing them closer to the dreams they have for their lives after graduation? How can they become even more effective in achieving that goal? How will the university's focus on research improve their community or the world? How will members of the faculty and staff engage their communities in new and innovative ways?

While it may be true that it's rarely the A Team itself that makes decisions about what goes into the school's mission and vision statements, it's also true that members of successful fundraising teams care very deeply about these issues. They make their voices heard and are often regarded as opinion leaders at the institution. A Teams have a vested interest in any discussion or decision about long-range planning. After all, it's the mission and vision of the entire institution that will help guide them in the gifts that they'll pursue.

So, they'll want to make sure that these goals are sufficiently meaningful and that the guiding documents of the institution—the mission and vision statements, strategic plan, and so on—provide the type of direction that will help their fundraising efforts be successful. For an overview of what AOs and DOs need to know about one another, see Appendix I.

THE STARS APPROACH

As vital as understanding the goal, focus, and rationale of what the institution is trying to accomplish through its advancement work, it's really only the beginning of the A Team's strategy. Effective academic fundraisers often follow a technique that we call the *STARS Approach* from an acronym based on five key elements:

- *S*trategy
- *T*eamwork
- *A*wareness
- *R*elationship
- *S*tewardship

STRATEGY

When we speak of strategy as an essential component of how A Teams work effectively together, we're thinking of two types of strategy that must be in place simultaneously: organizational strategy and fundraising strategy. *Organizational strategy* can be envisioned as the three parts of every successful journey:

1. *Destination. Where the university, college, or department intends to go.*
2. *Route. How it intends to get there.*
3. *Timetable. When it intends to arrive.*

At the institutional level, organizational strategy is usually outlined in a formal strategic plan. As we saw in Figure 1.2, that plan then guides the strategic thinking of each subsequent level of the university. So, if the A Team is working at the presidential level, it's likely to be focusing on the major strategic themes or goals of the institution.

Development teams at the level of the college, department, or program, however, will be pursuing goals that are specific to their areas, even though these goals remain well aligned with the institution's overall plan. If that practice isn't followed—for instance, if a biology department at a small teaching-centered, liberal arts college goes off on its own and starts raising funds for a graduate research facility—the institution's identity can become obscured for potential donors and future fundraising efforts for key priorities may become far more difficult.

An A Team makes it a practice to hold regular discussions about the strategic direction of the institution and how its current fundraising plans fit into that larger effort. In that way, if any member of the team is asked why the project they're pursuing is beneficial to the school as a whole, that person can relate the team's effort to institutional mission and vision, illustrating the greater good that will occur if the request is funded.

It's common practice for colleges and universities to develop strategic plans that will guide them for at least the next decade. Nevertheless, in reality, the further a strategic plan projects into the future, the less valuable it is as a guide. There are simply too many unforeseen factors in higher education for very-long-range plans to be reliable.

For instance, few academic administrators understood in the early 1990s how the Internet would become a major factor in higher education only a few years later. Few people understood as late as the first half of 2007 how the economic downturn known as the Great Recession would affect colleges, universities, and community colleges for the next five to ten years.

The point is not that we should stop planning, but that A Teams should be realistic about what they present to donors about their program's future. Our general rule of thumb is that *strategic plans can provide specific guidance for only about three to five years into the future*. Beyond that five-year window, a strategic plan can describe general hopes and anticipated directions, but is less useful in providing reliable indicators of where the college or university is likely to be at any specific point in time.

In other words, A Teams complement their strategic planning with the strategies of *scenario planning* and *setting a strategic compass*: building the infrastructure of their institution or program so that it can be resilient and take advantage of *whatever* scenario the future may bring (see Buller, 2015, 119–126).

In short, strategic planning is about setting directions and determining pathways; scenario planning and setting a strategic compass are about building strong foundations. What A Teams know that other groups may overlook is that effective fundraising only occurs when you pay attention to both.

The second type of strategy A Teams consider, *fundraising strategy*, involves finding connections between the institution's fundraising *needs* (as established by its organizational strategy) and the *ability* of external constituents to meet those needs. In formulating a fundraising strategy, the team will explore various prospects, consider how each might be connected to one or more institutional needs, and plan the most effective way to present their ideas to the prospect.

For instance, did someone make a donation in the past for a similar purpose? Was the person a graduate of the program? Is the person's spouse interested in the area served by the program? Does the person's record of philanthropy indicate similar interests? And what is this person's financial capacity or record of giving to comparable causes?

Fundraising strategy thus explores how individual donors and foundations may be connected to any given project, but it also looks at how the total financial needs of the project can be addressed. To do so, the team calculates the projected cost of the project, subdivides that cost into several different giving levels, and then determines how many gifts at each level it will need to pursue.

The result is what is known as a *gift pyramid*: a visual outline of the number of donations needed at each level of giving. Since most projects receive far more small gifts than large gifts, the overall form of this plan usually takes on a triangular shape. In designing its gift pyramid, the team needs to establish

- The amount of giving it can reasonably expect at each level of the pyramid.
- The total number of gifts that would be needed at that level.
- The probable number of prospects the team will need to cultivate in order to achieve its required number of gifts at each level.
- The percentage of its overall goal that the team believes it can raise at each level.

The general rule of thumb is that you should always be able to *identify at least 4–5 times the number of prospects needed for each gift at each level*, with this number increased in difficult economic times or for projects that are likely to have only a limited appeal.

In order to see how a gift pyramid works, let's suppose you want to pursue a project that will require $10 million in external funding, but you think it's highly unlikely that a single donor will provide that entire amount. Suppose, too, that the largest individual gift made by any of your program's donors to date has been just under $2 million. Because of the importance of the current project, you think you may be able to persuade one of those large donors to contribute a bit more than he or she did in the past, but not substantially more.

In such a case, your gift pyramid might end up looking like the one seen in Figure 1.3. Of course, like long-range strategic plans, a gift pyramid is highly

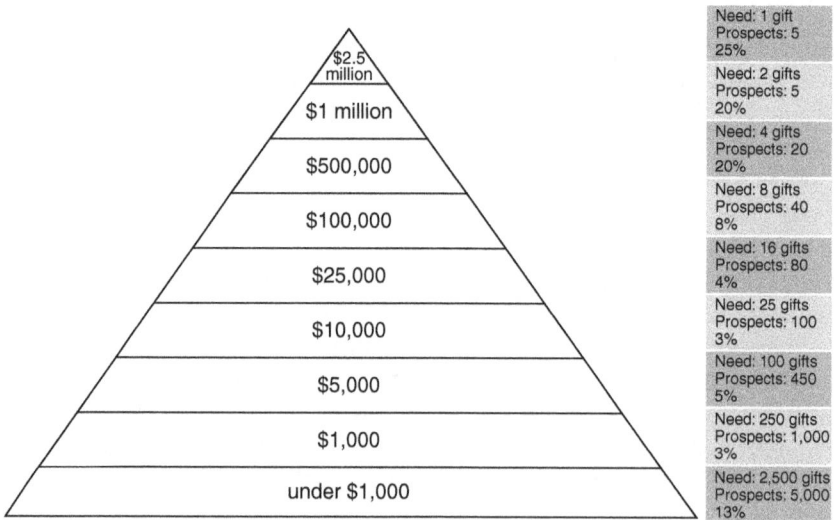

Figure 1.3.   A Sample Gift Pyramid.

unlikely to be funded precisely as it was designed. Rather than receiving two million dollar gifts and eight gifts in the $100,000 range, you may end up with only one million-dollar gift and fifteen in the $100,000 range. But the gift pyramid gives you a starting point so that you can determine whether your fundraising strategy is even feasible.

In some cases, too, you may discover that the gifts you're likely to receive don't fit easily into this familiar pyramid. For example, you may be working in an environment that is financially very bimodal, with donors available at the very top and very bottom ranges of your plan, but with relatively few prospects in the middle.

In this case, your gift pyramid might look more like a "gift hourglass," but it will still help you set your strategy for moving forward. In a similar way, there may be situations in which you conclude that the vast majority of the funding you need is likely to come from your largest donors, with only a tiny percentage contributed through small gifts. The result would be an "inverted gift pyramid."

So, what we'll refer to as gift pyramids for the sake of convenience can actually assume several shapes. But, as you can tell from the number of donors listed at each level of giving in the program of the next concert or play you attend, the traditional triangular shape is by far the most common form gifts to any cause assume.

Regardless of its precise shape, however, the gift pyramid should always be an important component of the A Team's fundraising strategy. It helps the team understand where its efforts need to begin and what types of gift (pledges, endowments, expendable funds, and so on) it'll need to pursue. For our hypothetical $10 million project, for example, the three top levels account for 65% of the group's overall goal, even though they consist of only seven gifts. It becomes very clear, therefore, that a significant portion of time will have to be devoted to pursuing those seven gifts.

Moreover, if the team can persuade a donor at one of the top two or three levels to commit to this project early in its efforts, that donation becomes a *lead gift*: a contribution that helps inspire others to contribute to the same cause. Donors who provide lead gifts frequently become your strongest supporters in promoting the project to other contributors. They become honorary members of your A Team. After all, they don't want their gift to be wasted; they thus take a great deal of ownership in making the project succeed and can make very forceful arguments like, "I've already given a rather substantial gift because I really believe in the importance of this work. Won't you join with me in contributing at whatever level you can?"

Finally, it's important to realize that you don't have to reinvent the wheel when you wish to establish a gift pyramid. A number of formulas and calculators are available that can make your planning of a mini-campaign much easier. You simply enter your target amount, and the gift range calculator develops an initial gift pyramid, which you can then modify according to your understanding of your donor base. For sample gift pyramid calculators, see Blackbaud's Gift Range Calculator (blackbaud. com/company/resources/giftrange/giftcalc.aspx.), Alexander Macnab and Company's Gift Table Calculator (alexandermacnab.com/get-started/calcu-lator/), and FundRaisingcoach.com and TheNonprofitAcademy.com's Gift Range Calculator (giftrangecalculator.com).

After your gift pyramid has been prepared, your next step is to identify prospective donors for each category of giving. You'll discover some of these prospects through third party introductions, inquiries people have made to your newsletter or website, letters written to the unit by people who want to know more about what it does, contacts made by members of your area's advisory board, online sources like fundsnetservices.com and foundation-center.org, and names you encounter via social media such as Facebook and Twitter.

While some of these ways of meeting prospective donors are free, there's no escaping that old adage that "It takes money to make money." Many fundraising efforts have failed because the institution wasn't willing to fund the up-front costs required to mount a successful development strategy. Your fundraising budget may need to include funds for travel, meals and entertain-ment, and even gifts or tokens of appreciation.

At most state-supported institutions there will be strict policies about what can and cannot be paid for with government-provided funds, that part of a program's budget that's often labeled *E&G* for *Education and General Funds*. In the pages that follow, we'll assume that your college or university already has all the necessary support areas in place, such as the capacity to perform donor research, access to the professional expertise needed to execute planned giving agreements, and a functional prospect/donor manage-ment database.

If these fundamental requirements aren't yet in place at your school, then you're not yet ready for most of what we'll be discussing in the next section. Go back and pick up a resource like Hunt (2012), Sargeant and Shang (2010), or Ciconte and Jacob (2009), and make an effort to get the basics in place. Even so, it's important to remember that, although these resources are essen-tial, you'll never reach a point where your funding is enough to support all the things you'd *like* to do. Since time and other resources are short, it's always necessary to set priorities for your fundraising goals. Having everyone on the team aware of the overall strategy will help make those priorities clearer.

Once a number of prospective donors have been identified, it then becomes important to learn more about them, including their giving capacity, areas of achievement, past and current philanthropic interests, and possible connections to the project under consideration. The development office will take the lead in determining the prospect's financial status, either formally with research and data mining programs (e.g., Sumac) and websites (e.g., aspireresearchgroup.com) or informally with information gleaned through personal relationships.

Since the list will almost always contain the names of alumni, past donors, current students and their parents, community leaders, and those who do business with the institution, other offices on campus may also be able to provide you with valuable insights. That information can be used to determine the best way to cultivate each prospective donor. Common ways of initiating that process with someone include

- Having a current member of a governing or advisory board invite the prospect to lunch along with the academic administrator and DO.
- Sending a handwritten invitation to a special event, like an art opening, guest lecture, or sporting event.
- Visiting the prospect's office or home in order to provide an update on recent activities in your area.
- Offering the prospect an opportunity to visit a meeting of your advisory board in order to see if he or she would consider joining.

Any of those approaches requires a substantial investment of time; so you'll want to take full advantage of the second element in the STARS approach: Teamwork.

TEAMWORK

Since we're talking about strategies for creating an A Team, it may seem redundant to emphasize how important it is to develop teamwork. But we're not talking about the sort of teamwork that exists when people just work together professionally and collegially. What we have in mind is the sort of teamwork that exists at a far deeper level, a type of interaction that we call *maximum collegial flow* (see Buller, 2013, 48–53). Everyone has experienced that mental state that psychologists like Csíkszentmihályi (1990) refer to as *flow*: the point at which you're so absorbed in an activity that you lose all track of time and effort.

But it's not just individuals who can become totally immersed in an activity; groups can experience a sense of flow, too. That perfect level of teamwork that we're calling maximum collegial flow occurs when a group is functioning smoothly, effectively, and with near perfect harmony. We see maximum collegial flow in an athletic team that's "in the zone," a string quartet that's performing at its peak, and a group of friends who are so in tune with one another that they can finish each other's sentences.

That's how an A Team functions, perhaps not 100% of the time, but so often that it can be regarded as its standard operating procedure. Sometimes maximum collegial flow develops spontaneously. The members of the team just "click," and their working relationship is smooth and productive from the very beginning. At other times, however, this level of effectiveness arises only after members of the group invest a good deal of effort. In that case, it may be several years before the team feels that it's connecting at the highest possible level and everyone's "on the same page" about its goals, tasks, and methods.

Nearly everything we discuss in this book is directed towards developing this high level of teamwork among the members of your fundraising group. But one ingredient is important to establish right away. It's a trait that can be found in almost every A Team we've encountered: a high degree of *flexibility*.

Fundraising is a path with plenty of twists and turns, and you rarely end up at exactly the same destination you set out for. The best teamwork requires *adaptability* and *dynamism*, the willingness to take advantage of unexpected opportunities when they arise and the ability to recover quickly from disappointments when they occur.

You may have heard that the first rule of improvisational comedy is develop a "Yes, and …" mindset. In other words, if another member of the troupe hands you a glass of water and tells you, "I've found it! This is the elixir of eternal life," the worst thing you can possibly do is reply, "No, it isn't. It's just a glass of water." In order to keep the improvisation going, you have to accept whatever premise you've just been given. For example, you might drink the entire glass of water, look at your partner in a puzzled manner, and say, "What? You saved some for yourself, right?"

That same type of synergistic give-and-take is part of what makes an A Team effective. Imagine, for instance, you're meeting with a donor whose entire career has been focused on starting new businesses, and so you've planned to talk about starting a new center for entrepreneurship at your university. If the prospect says, "Well, ever since my granddaughter got accepted into Juilliard, I've really been more interested in opera than business," it does little good to say, "Oh, sorry. Our mistake."

If your colleague on the team says something like, "In that case I'll think you'll be excited about what we've got in mind for the performing arts at our school," don't undermine his or her effort by saying, "What are you talking about? You haven't mentioned anything like that before." Remember the rule of improvisational comedy and say instead, "Yes, and you're just the sort of person who can make a real difference in that initiative."

In the long run, a "Yes, and ..." mentality with a donor who's unexpectedly interested in a performing arts center is your most effective strategy even if you're the dean of a business college and realize that another unit will now be benefiting from this gift. Donors usually don't see the academic silos we take for granted. In most cases, they assume that the business dean is a strong supporter of the arts program, and that the performing arts dean backs the business program 100%.

Besides it's not just with your own DO that you want to create an A Team relationship; it's with your colleagues on the council of deans as well. Do a good deed for another program today, and it becomes much more likely that your fellow dean will do something to help you tomorrow.

Of course, effective teamwork doesn't mean that *all* your cultivating and fundraising activities have to be done as a group. There are prospects who would feel intimidated talking to a university president, just as there are other prospects who would be turned off by the presence of a DO at the very first meeting. Another important rule of thumb is that *being part of an A Team means understanding when one of your partners needs to "fly solo."*

Administrators who feel offended by a prospective donor's reluctance to meet with them don't understand that the most effective approach in this situation would be to hang back a little. DOs who insist on being in on the "ground floor" for every conversation a chair or dean has with a member of the community may be depriving themselves of significant contributions a few months or years in the future. The key to teamwork, in short, is *trust*. You can hardly expect a prospective donor to trust the members of a team if they don't appear to trust one another.

While initial meetings with individual donors are sometimes best handled one-on-one, proposals made to foundations or corporations almost always require the presence of the full team. The foundation or company itself is likely to send a group to the meeting and to have questions that will probably go beyond the expertise of one individual.

In addition, the availability of your A Team from the very beginning saves time and provides for speedier follow-up. Each member will come away with the action items for which he or she is immediately responsible and will understand the best possible way of getting answers to any questions that remain.

AWARENESS

One of the reasons why A Teams are able to develop maximum collegial flow is that they're aware of the personalities, skills, and shortcomings of every member of the group. But A Teams also achieve a high level of awareness in three other areas as well:

1. Awareness of the project.
2. Awareness of the donor.
3. Awareness of the community.

Let's explore each of these topics individually.

Awareness of the project consists of a candid recognition of the extent and limit of each project and the reasons its success is important. Notice that word *candid*. There's a huge difference between the questions "Why are we doing this?" and "Why are we *really* doing this?"

The first question is often answered in terms of the type of mission and vision statements we explored earlier. It's the message intended for public consumption. "We're interested in this project because we've long been committed to the quality of undergraduate education. A great deal of research has demonstrated that undergraduate students who become engaged in research projects early in their career are more likely to persist in college, learn better, and be competitive in the job market after they graduate. That's why we have this initiative promoting undergraduate research."

Those are all wonderful reasons for pursuing external funding, and the school is certainly being honest when it describes these to potential donors. But there are also *internal* reasons for seeking external funding.

For instance, the college or university may need to build its scholarship fund so that it can remain competitive with its peer institutions when it recruits the best students. It may simply be responding to an opportunity (perhaps someone at the institution found out about a wealthy member of the community with a strong interest in undergraduate research) that seemed too good to pass up. It may be seeking funds that are *budget relieving*: the sort of revenue that allows current resources to be redirected toward other priorities. It may simply need the funding to balance its budget. Or there may be many other reasons.

The point is that each member of the team needs to be aware, not just of the stated reasons for the project, but also of these underlying, more candid reasons. One of the themes we're trying to underscore throughout this book is that fundraising projects almost always evolve over their cultivation periods. It's very rare for any idea to be funded by a donor at the full amount in exactly the way that the project was first proposed. Donors have their own interests that they want reflected in the final proposal, and many donors are astute investors—after all, that's how many of them made their money—and so will easily spot ways in which they believe a project can be made more effective.

By being aware of the "real" reasons for the proposal, all members of the team understand what's negotiable and what's absolutely essential for achieving the institution's ultimate goal. For example, a project that was originally intended to increase scholarship funding could easily become a financial burden for the institution if the donor wants all scholarship funds eliminated from the proposal and wishes instead to provide a year or two of start-up funding for a new academic discipline.

If after this initial period the school will become liable for funding the project for many years to come, it has created a new problem for itself without solving the old one. It's now on the hook for a program it didn't really want, while it still doesn't have the scholarship funding it needs. We refer to a project of this sort as *a gift that keeps on taking*. At their most innocuous, these missteps are mere inconveniences. But at their worst, such gifts become "black holes" for resources, diverting funding that's desperately needed in other areas. By being fully aware of what the goals for a project *really* are, the A Team brings the institution closer to its goals and scrupulously avoids taking on burdens that will cause the school to lose momentum.

The second type of awareness characteristic of A Teams is their *awareness of the donor*. Earlier we discussed the importance of knowing a donor's philanthropic interests and capacity for giving and the Three Ds that characterize effective mission and vision statements. A Teams certainly cover those bases in their preparation, but they're also aware of the *Three Ps*: the prospective donor's *personality*, *pursuits*, and *passions*.

For example, will frequent visits make the person feel valued or badgered? Is it better to call, text, email, or send a handwritten letter? Are trips to the opera or a NASCAR rally likely to be more welcome? At what time of day is the prospect best reached? What are the person's "third rails," the topics you should never, ever touch? Depending on their situations, different donors might respond in completely different ways to cultivation efforts that address their

- *Tax advantages*. Prospects who have substantial resources are often interested in how their philanthropic gifts can help them pursue an important social goal at the same time that it reduces their tax liability. If you're the dean of the business school, you'll have faculty members with this expertise readily available. But what if you're the dean of humanities or the DO for a nursing program? In these cases, you'll want to work closely with a legal or financial advisor. You'll need to have detailed information available about the tax advantages of trusts, deferred gifts, gifts-in-kind, and other types of philanthropic "products" so that you can provide a useful service to the donor at the same time that you benefit your own program.

- *Prestige*. Other prospects may care relatively little about the money they can save through tax advantages but be highly motivated by the opportunity to see their names on buildings or scholarships. With these donors, the A Team has to be aware of what it means for someone to *build a legacy*. Most schools have very explicit policies about naming opportunities (dealing with such questions as "What's the minimal acceptable gift?" and "Can facilities be named after people who are still alive?").

  While the DO will certainly be aware of these policies, it's important for *every* member of the team to understand them so that no one inadvertently offers—or even *appears* to offer—more than the institution can really provide. In addition, there may be other naming opportunities that require smaller gifts; some of these opportunities may be more affordable because they deal with parts of a building rather than the entire structure (such as an auditorium rather than a center for the performing arts) or more limited in time (such as naming rights for a decade rather than in perpetuity).

  You could also explore the possibility of granting the donor naming rights to a specific event (such as "the Jordan P. Wright Lecture in Multimedia Studies"), award ("the Jordan P. Wright Prize in Entrepreneurial Achievement"), or scholarship ("the Jordan P. Wright Fellow in Applied Linguistics").

  No matter what form they take, naming rights should never be sold too inexpensively, and every possible contingency should be explored. For example, what happens to the unit's name if it splits into multiple parts or is otherwise reorganized, dissolved, or absorbed by another discipline?

- *Benefits and Perks*. There are also donors who are most interested in renewing or increasing their contribution because of special favors or services your program can provide. A *Frequent Friends Program* that provides donors who have contributed to the annual fund for at least ten consecutive years could offer listing of their names in the program of each event sponsored by the program, special seating and opportunities to meet the speaker for each major lecture, escorted transportation from a reserved parking space to campus activities, and the like.

  Benefits can be increased based on the length of the donor's affiliation with the program, the size of the gift, the number of times the donor's level of giving has increased, or any other factor deemed appropriate for your program.

It's particularly important for members of the team who have academic backgrounds to be aware of these motivations. As we've already seen, faculty members occasionally have trouble understanding that donors don't give money just because the program *needs* it; they give money because they want to see some kind of *result*. That result might be as self-serving as seeing their name on a stadium or as altruistic as engaging in what is known in Hebrew as *tikkun olam*: repairing the world.

In other words, some people engage in philanthropy simply because of the good feeling it gives them, while others want to be viewed as important, still others want to alleviate a type of suffering that has affected them in some way, and some people just take pleasure in seeing others happy. There's no single profile of the academic philanthropist, and that's why successful fundraising usually requires every member of the team to be aware of "what makes the donor tick."

In *The Seven Faces of Philanthropy*, Prince and File (2001) suggest that there are several basic types of donors:

1. *Communitarian.* The donor, usually with a business background, who wants to keep gifts in the community in which he or she works.
2. *Devout.* The donor who believes that giving is a moral obligation and is part of God's will.
3. *Socialite.* The donor who enjoys having fun while doing good for others and who will work within or expand his or her own social network.
4. *Investor.* The donor who uses charitable donations as part of a personal estate tax-planning strategy.
5. *Altruist.* The donor who does not seek publicity, but wants to help those with the greatest needs.
6. *Repayer.* The donor who wants to give back, frequently to organizations by which he or she was helped in the past, such as a school or hospital.
7. *Dynast.* The donor who was groomed from generations of giving within his or her family. This type of donor wants to continue the family tradition of philanthropy.

The third type of awareness, *awareness of the community*, helps the A Team identify opportunities they might miss if all the members were just working independently. Each member of the team has a chance to learn about new prospects by attending community events, such as chamber of commerce meetings or luncheons held by service organizations, and they can pass on what they learn to other members of the team or even (where appropriate) to other teams.

Having different backgrounds and social networks helps in this respect. The administrator is likely to gain information from students and faculty members that the DO wouldn't otherwise learn. The DO might learn something from a fellow member of a civic organization or country club that the academic administrator didn't know. The team approach thus brings additional eyes and ears to a process for which information is key, especially information relevant to our next ingredient in the STARS Approach: building relationships.

RELATIONSHIPS

Of all the elements that form the STARS Approach, building relationships is probably second in importance only to developing an overall strategy. To put it simply, fundraising is all about relationships. It's not a transactional process based on a simple *quid pro quo* where the most critical factor is how soon you "close the deal." Rather it develops organically out of the relationships you build with external stakeholders and how those relationships grow over time.

Particularly when larger gifts are involved, members of an A Team understand the role that patience has to play in the process. Every member of the team needs to have excellent social and communication skills, always remembering that effective communication involves *listening* as well as *speaking*.

The relationships you build through fundraising can be the most rewarding part of your entire development effort. As the author and fundraising consultant Ken Burnett says,

> Relationship fundraising can show you how to avoid making mistakes in dealing with donors, how to avoid wasting money and how to make your promotion pay, how to increase your donors' annual giving and extend their "life" as donors, how to manage your staff and present your organization, how to approach your marketing strategy, how to make your donor your friend, how to increase the value of your donors and how to ensure a gigantic leap in your income from bequests (also known as legacies). It can also be very satisfying and rewarding. (Burnett, 2002, 42–43)

Even though it's important for all members of the team to be adept at building relationships, it's a simple fact that the lion's share of building most fundraising relationships falls on the development member(s) of the team.

The profession of DO tends to attract people who are very sociable in their nature, endowed with an outgoing and pleasant demeanor, and willing to invest time and effort to a process that may come to fruition only years later. While it's wonderful if those same attributes are shared by everyone else on the team, chairs, deans, and presidents simply don't have time to build as many deep external relationships as the DO does. As a result, what the administrator can do periodically, the DO does consistently.

A prospect who's treated well and respectfully may remain a lifelong supporter of the program, perhaps even leaving a legacy gift that can be utterly transformative for that discipline. However, a person who feels slighted, neglected, or taken advantage of may quickly change from being one of the program's closest friends to being one of its sharpest critics; it can take years to repair the relationship in these cases.

Let's explore an actual incident that happened to Dianne, one of the co-authors of this book. She'd been working with a prospect for two years, getting to know her interests and looking for ways in which those interests might match those of the college she was representing. In order to deepen this relationship, Dianne thought it might be a good idea for this donor to sit down with the president of the university so that they could each learn a bit about one another's background. She briefed the president that the lunch would just be a "get-to-know-you meeting" and that there was a long process ahead before they'd be ready to ask the prospect for a sizable gift. But within moments of meeting the donor, the president said, "It's very nice to meet you, and your interest in marine science is near and dear to our hearts. I really hope that you'll be able to support our efforts with two million dollars to support a professorship that we'll name after you."

The prospect was aghast and took a few moments before recovering her composure. She soon made an excuse to cut short the meeting and, after the president had left, asked Dianne if she knew that the president was going to request money in this way. The question left Dianne in an awkward position: Because of her position, she had to defend the president, and yet she was equally as caught off-guard by the sudden request as the prospect had been. All she could think of to say was, "I think the president is so enthusiastic about this new project that perhaps he's a little overzealous in attempting to secure funding for it."

But the damage had already been done. By not taking time to build a relationship with this prospect, the president alienated her and, even though Dianne tried for several years to renew their conversation, the potential donor never again wanted anything to do with the university.

This cautionary tale is particularly important to keep in mind because we live in an age of instant communication. It's now possible, with just a few keystrokes, to obtain long lists of people who have the financial resources to make a substantial gift to the institution. But building relationships is a part of fundraising where *quality always takes precedence over quantity.* A few small gifts may result from email blasts, quick asks at initial meetings, or DONATE buttons on the school's website, but truly transformative gifts will almost always result from long, highly personal cultivation processes.

Members of an A Team understand the need for relationships to grow and mature. They trust what other members of the team tell them regarding when the time is right to bring up various issues. In fact, once A Teams have been working together for several years, they rarely even have to express these sentiments in words: A glance or a tone of voice is all the other members need to know in order to determine whether it's the right time for an ask—or not.

STEWARDSHIP

If the relationship with a donor frequently begins many years before a large gift is made, it doesn't end once the ink is dry on the check. The receipt of the gift itself should be thought of not as a period, but as a comma in the relationship. From a financial perspective, that single gift may well lead to several others if the donor continues to be cultivated effectively.

From an ethical standpoint, you now owe it to that donor to make sure that his or her wishes are honored and the benefits accruing from the donation are reported to the one person who made it all possible. This process of extending and improving donor relationships after a gift has been made is called *stewardship*, and it includes

- The prudent investment and management of funds.
- Accurate and transparent reporting of how those funds are used.
- Making sure that the donor is included in reports on the project, as well as other activities that may be of interest.
- Giving the donor an opportunity to meet those who benefited from the gift, where appropriate.
- Any other contacts or activities that help the donor feel as involved in the project as he or she still wants to be.

In addition to making sure that the donor feels properly thanked for the contribution that he or she has made, good stewardship involves respecting his or her privacy and rights. Some donors like to be "made over" and treated as a constant object of attention; some prefer to remain anonymous. And A Teams are wise enough to discern the difference.

That attribute of awareness we discussed earlier helps the team make sure that only the *right* sort of attention is paid to any given donor. You don't want to mortify a shy donor with a splashy public event any more than you want to ignore a gregarious donor who can't see his or her name publicized too often. Good prospect research involves far more than determining a person's giving capacity; it also involves finding out the person's preferences in a wide range of areas.

An effective steward of a philanthropic gift understands that the motivation for giving often changes over time as a person's life changes due to different experiences, such as tragedies or additions to the family. He or she will also understand that a person's attitude toward giving may be shaped by his or her faith, ethnic background, and current view of the world. You don't want to engage in stereotypes—"All Democrats are bleeding hearts, and all Republicans are members of the NRA."—but neither do you want to be unaware of an aspect of someone's background that may shape his or her philanthropic focus.

Workshops and training programs are widely available in many areas of fundraising such as identification of potential donors, effective methods of cultivation, and appropriate ways of making the ask. But you rarely see training programs devoted to stewardship, which is unfortunate in light of how important this topic is to donor relations. So, if you want the members of your A Team to embrace stewardship as completely as it embraces other aspects of their duties, we recommend a five-step plan.

Step 1. Make sure that your list of donors who have already made gifts to your program is accurate and up to date.

Particularly if you're new to an institution, you may not be aware of all the donors who have previously made gifts to your area. Check the files of both the academic discipline and the development office to make sure you know about all relevant gift agreements and other substantial contributions that were made to your program. What counts as a "substantial" contribution will vary considerably across disciplines and institutions. A gift of $1,000 may be regarded as a routine contribution to the Annual Fund at one school but seen as a sizable gift at another.

Regardless of how you define large gifts, your stewardship of them won't get very far if you don't know who your benefactors are, how many are still living, when they were last contacted by the institution, and what sort of contacts they've been receiving.

In other words, have they simply been receiving a copy of the university magazine? Were subsequent solicitations made? Was the person ever formally thanked for his or her gift? Have regular updates about the impact of the gift been provided? What, in short, has been the institution's past record of stewardship with regard to each significant gift?

Step 2. Have the A Team reach out to all living donors, beginning with those who have not been contacted in some time.

Once you've obtained this information, begin contacting all living donors. The DO on the team should know whether any other units of the school have also been contacting that donor. You don't want two sides of the institution to work against one another by appearing to solicit different types of gifts. The awareness component of the STARS Approach will mean that you know whether it's preferable to contact a particular donor with a personal visit rather than a phone call, a written note rather than an email message, a formal letter rather than an informal card, and so on.

In most cases, your initial message will be simple: As an advocate for your area, you think it's important to keep all of the discipline's donors up to date about what's going on in the program. If you can provide any stories of specific benefits that have resulted from the donor's gift, that information will always be beneficial. Perhaps there's a particular student who benefited from the scholarship that the donor made possible, or there may be a speaker who was brought to campus because of this person's generosity. Be as specific as you can in describing the benefits that resulted from the gift, express your gratitude warmly, and answer any questions that the donor may have.

As you engage in this process, you may discover that some donors feel they've been neglected in the past. When that occurs, it's possible that you'll endure some anger for what the donors regard as prior indifference. Listen to the donor graciously. Apologize for any neglect for which you yourself were responsible. Explain that you can't speak for people who held your position earlier, but you regard donors as one of the most important resources the institution has. Invite the donor to campus events. Meet informally over lunch, if this type of meeting seems appropriate.

Understand that, particularly when the donor feels that he or she has been ignored for a while, it might take a number of visits to "mend the fences." The donor may be testing you to see if you, too, will lose interest after one or two initial contacts. Be persistent, but don't be a pest. Try to find a rhythm that suits the need of the donor while demonstrating how much your program genuinely values that person's prior support.

In cases where a donor is no longer living, the research staff in the advancement office should try to track down that person's heirs. In most cases, these heirs will welcome hearing about what a difference their relative made to your program. While it's frequently the case that heirs will have other philanthropic interests and may not consider requests for future funding, there are also times when heirs will want to leave a memorial to their deceased relative. For this reason, regardless of whether contacting heirs results in further gifts or merely a good feeling on the part of the family, it's almost always beneficial to reach out to the person's children, grandchildren, or siblings.

Step 3. Continue providing the donors with current information about how their gifts are transforming lives.

Good stewardship doesn't involve just a single contact or effort. It's the result of renewed, consistent attention to the needs of the donor. One of the most effective ways for the A Team to keep in touch with donors is to provide consistent updates on the impact that their gifts have had on the institution and its programs.

For example, if the donor is responsible for a scholarship fund, it's likely that one or more new students will benefit from this program each year. A letter from you, along with a hand-written note from one of these students, can help remind the donor why that gift was important and demonstrate that you're using these funds precisely as he or she intended.

If the donor is responsible for underwriting a lecture series, the speaker may be willing to take a few minutes for an individual meeting with the donor. Even if that's not possible, you can send the donor details about how attendance at this program is increasing, the exposure the event is receiving in local newspapers, or copies of letters or emails you've received from people thanking you for the event.

Other types of updates can also be beneficial. A student could call and tell the donor what he or she learned from the speaker. If the contribution supported a faculty development or research fund, update the donor on the new projects that were funded. The donor isn't likely to see a scholarly article that appeared in a professional journal, but the professor could send an autographed offprint to the donor or make a call to summarize the significance of the project.

In short, donors want to know that their gifts had an *impact*. Members of an A Team are always on the lookout for where this type of impact occurs, and they keep the donors informed of what they discover. Doing so not only makes future gifts more likely, but it's also a professional and appropriate way to ensure that those who have helped the college or university in the past are treated respectfully and attentively.

Step 4. Explore ways in which you can re-engage past donors with the present activities of your program.

Even though good stewardship is the ethically proper thing to do, it would be disingenuous to ignore the practical side of responsible stewardship: It's an effective strategy for new contributions. After all, most people are more likely to contribute to a cause they already know, particularly when they're persuaded that their previous gifts have been used wisely. So, as you improve your relationship with past donors, you're also always laying the groundwork for possible additional gifts.

If there are campus events—such as public lectures, open house evenings, or faculty receptions—to which you can invite past donors, you should certainly do so. Even if the donors can't attend, they'll be pleased you made the effort to include them. The best practice, in fact, is to invite these past donors personally, either through a telephone call or a handwritten note. Doing so reinforces for the donors how important they are to the ongoing work of the institution and demonstrates your continued appreciation for their gift.

Your renewed contact with a past donor may also give you insight into further areas in which that individual may wish to help the university. For example, if the donor is particularly impressed by a lecture series that's struggling for support because it depends on a very limited departmental operating budget, he or she may decide to underwrite the series. If the donor meets a number of your students and comes to admire the quality of their work, he or she may decide to provide additional scholarship aid.

Your goal, in other words, should always be to leave the impression that your program has two traits simultaneously: (1) It enjoys a great deal of success right now (no one likes to contribute to a program that seems on the verge of failure) and (2) It could do even greater things if only additional funding were available (no one likes to contribute to a program that already seems to have all it needs). That can be a difficult balance to achieve, and it's one of the reasons for adopting a team approach rather than going it alone: The academic representatives are free to emphasize current successes, while the development representatives focus on current needs.

Step 5. Develop a systematic strategy for maintaining donor contact.

The last S in the STARS Approach brings us back to the first. Stewardship helps mold the strategy of the future. In fact, it becomes a central feature of that strategy because it causes you to remain in frequent contact with your donor base. Here are just a few of the ways in which you can maintain donor contact and thus help promote commitment to your school and its programs:

- Arrange to meet a donor who lives at some distance from campus whenever you're in that area for a conference, vacation, or a call to other donors. Even if you only stop by to say hello, these meetings can have a positive impact.
- Phone an out-of-state donor when you happen to be in that person's state, but a personal visit is not practical. For instance, you may be attending an event in the southern part of the state while the donor lives in the northern part, but you can still call to "touch base" since you "happen to be in the area."
- Send postcards to past donors anytime you travel to interesting places, including a note saying that some experience you had made you think of them. Bringing a set of preaddressed address labels with you on your travels simplifies this task.
- Set aside ten minutes every day to jot one note to one donor about what's going on in your program. After you've adopted this practice for a few weeks, you'll discover that you can create an interesting, personalized, and thoughtful message in a very short amount of time.
- Automatically include donors on all email lists that promote current events and activities in your area.

- Offer to provide speakers on current research to any service organizations of which the donor may be a member. Service organizations are always looking for new speakers, and philanthropic individuals frequently belong to several of these groups at once.

By doing the donor this favor, you're thanking that person in a very tangible way for his or her support, doing the donor a good service in return, and reminding the donor of the important work that's performed in your program. An added advantage is that this speaking engagement may also introduce you to other potential donors, thus increasing your pool of prospects.

- Create a section of your program's website that can be accessed only by donors who have received a special password. Update this site often, perhaps with a weekly note about current activities at the university. (If you're too busy to do this yourself, hire a student worker to do so. The cost is low, and most students are quite familiar with the most effective ways to use social media.) Remind donors frequently of the website's existence through emails, notices in newsletters, mass mailings, and the like.

The single greatest complaint donors have about fundraising is that people contact them frequently when they want a gift but then ignore them entirely once the gift has been received. Effective stewardship helps you avoid this problem, treats each donor as a unique individual, and demonstrates gratitude in a manner that's meaningful to your most important supporters. A good rule of thumb is that if you have to choose between investing time in soliciting new donors or demonstrating gratitude to established donors, you should always devote your energies to the latter. Proper donor support is not only the right and honorable thing to do, but it's also often your most reliable way to secure future gifts to your program.

CASE STUDY

Your team has been cultivating a potential donor for quite some time. Throughout your discussions, the goal has been to seek an endowed professorship in Analytical Philosophy, an area where your program is crucially understaffed and where enrollment is climbing. In addition, this new faculty position will round out your philosophy program nicely, making it pre-eminent in the region. Ongoing budgetary challenges, however, mean that you're completely dependent on external funding for this position. You doubt if your university will ever be able to provide such a line out of its own resources.

You're just getting near the point at which you feel ready to make a formal ask when the prospect takes you by surprise. "You know," he begins, "my granddaughter was diagnosed with autism last year, and her condition has pretty much broken our hearts. It's all I can think of these days. I know when we started talking about a possible gift a year or so ago I was all interested in Analytical Philosophy since that was the field in which I did my own studies. But my priorities have changed. I want to endow a position in Autism Studies now. In fact, I'll write you a check today."

Your team works so well with one another that you all respond as though you'd been rehearsing your parts for a year. You express sympathy, agree that autism is a huge challenge, but note that Autism Studies doesn't really relate to the needs or mission of the university. You aren't even sure there's a program in which to place such a position. However, if the donor will fund the line in Analytical Philosophy, perhaps the school could consider hosting a regular public lecture about autism or bring in a panel of external speakers.

The donor is unfazed. "If you don't have a program in Autism Studies, then I say now's the time to start one. Let me put it this way: We were talking about a four-million-dollar gift to fund a single faculty line in philosophy. To get the new program going, I'll give you twelve million dollars for *three* lines in Autism Studies, along with enough operating capital to start the program right away. But if you're only interested in Analytical Philosophy, then I'll write you a check for $50,000. You can hire a temporary instructor for maybe one year, and then we're through. So, which is it?"

You realize that the donor is serious and is expecting an answer right away.

Question: What do you do?

POSSIBLE STRATEGIES

Perhaps your safest strategy at this point is to acknowledge and appreciate the donor's shift in priorities while seeking to buy some time before a full response is given. Since the team has worked with this prospect for quite some time, they already have a good relationship with him.

Begin by recognizing that the situation has changed. For example, the DO might respond by saying, "We can certainly understand your passion about Autism Studies, and we wish your granddaughter success in her therapies in the future. Your offer of a twelve-million-dollar gift is so generous that it requires serious consideration on our part. There are many implications involved with establishing a new program, and we respectfully request some time to consider whether there's any way for us to incorporate this area of teaching and research into the academic priorities of the institution. Would you please give us a week to review this opportunity?"

This response does two things: It buys the team some time to determine the best possible way of proceeding, and it demonstrates good common sense when suddenly confronted with a large potential gift in an unexpected area. Any gift of this magnitude is going to require review to make sure that it really does fit into the mission of the college or university. Otherwise, it could easily become one of those "gifts that keeps on taking."

It also shows the prospective donor that the college is taking his request seriously and wants to give it due consideration. The outcome could go either way, but even if the college declines the magnanimous gift, the donor will realize that it gave thorough and careful consideration to the possibilities in light of the college's mission.

As discussions continue, maintain contact with the donor and gauge whether this new interest is a sincere change of focus or merely a sentiment of the moment. After all, a person who seems to have changed focus so quickly could, within a few weeks or months, change back again. So, even while you have serious discussions about whether a program in Autism Studies is appropriate for your mission, don't give up on the philosophy position totally.

Allow the process to take its natural course and, if it's eventually decided that a new autism program can't be a priority for the school, explain this decision diplomatically. In this manner it will leave the door open to a continued relationship with the donor, despite his claims that the $50,000 gift will be his final contribution.

CONCLUDING THOUGHTS

Members of A Teams are effective because they each understand one another, their ultimate goals, and the donors with whom they work. They share information freely, feel free to present differences of opinion candidly in private, and support one another publicly. The STARS Approach keeps the A Team on track by focusing their attention on their highest priorities and working collaboratively to achieve far greater results than any member of the team could hope for individually.

REFERENCES

Buller, J. L. (2013). *Positive academic leadership: How to stop putting out fires and begin making a difference*. San Francisco, CA: Jossey-Bass.

Buller, J. L. (2015). *Change leadership in higher education: A practical guide to academic transformation*. San Francisco, CA: Jossey-Bass.

Burnett, K. (2002). *Relationship fundraising: A donor-based approach to the business of raising money.* (2nd Ed.) San Francisco, CA: Jossey-Bass.

Ciconte, B. L., & Jacob, J. G. (2009). *Fundraising basics: A complete guide*. (3rd Ed.) Sudbury, MA: Jones and Bartlett Publishers.

Csíkszentmihályi, M. (1990). *Flow: The psychology of optimal experience*. New York, NY: Harper & Row.

Hunt, P. C. (2012). *Development for academic leaders: A practical guide for fundraising success*. San Francisco, CA: Jossey-Bass.

Prince, R. A., & File, K. M. (2001). *The seven faces of philanthropy: A new approach to cultivating major donors.* San Francisco, CA: Jossey-Bass.

Sargeant, A., & Shang, J. (2010). *Fundraising principles and practice.* San Francisco, CA: Jossey-Bass.

RESOURCES

Alexander, G. D., & Carlson, K. J. (2005). *Essential principles for fundraising success: An answer manual for the everyday challenges of raising money.* San Francisco, CA: Jossey-Bass.

Brinckerhoff, P. C. (2004). *Nonprofit stewardship: A better way to lead your mission-based organization.* Saint Paul, MN: Wilder Center for Communities.

Dove, K. E. (2001). *Conducting a successful fundraising program: A comprehensive guide and resource.* San Francisco, CA: Jossey-Bass.

Filla, J. J., & Brown, H. E. (2013). *Prospect research for fundraisers: The essential handbook.* Hoboken, NJ: John Wiley & Sons.

Hedrick, J. (2008). *Effective donor relations.* Hoboken, NJ: John Wiley & Sons.

Chapter Two

Responding as a Team
to Leadership Challenges

A Team, the term that we're using for your institution's most effective and elite group of fundraisers, may remind you of the 1980s television series *The A-Team* that starred George Peppard, Mr. T, Dirk Benedict, and many others. That fictional A-Team consisted of former U.S. Army Special Forces commandos who, falsely accused of a crime, hired themselves out as soldiers of fortune while trying to clear their names. There was no problem the A-Team couldn't solve and, even when the situation seemed impossible, it always found a way to succeed.

That level of proficiency was decidedly not seen in another fictional gang of misfits: the military unit assigned to Fort Courage in the 1960s series *F Troop*. The soldiers assigned to F Troop were the polar opposite of those in the A-Team. No task, however simple, seemed to be within their grasp. They were utter failures—lovable at times but failures nonetheless—and survived only because the neighboring Hekawi Indian tribe was equally inept.

We mention these two television series because, as you've undoubtedly found in your own experience, not everyone you meet in higher education development is A-Team material. We all have to deal with a few F-Troop types as well. In this chapter, therefore, we want to explore how the members of the A Team handle situations when their efforts are hindered, complicated, or flat-out undermined by an F Troop. There are dozens of things that can go wrong when you're trying to move from initial contact through cultivation and solicitation to stewardship and, unfortunately, many of your biggest challenges are going to be caused by human error or error-prone humans.

CHALLENGES CAUSED BY
INSTITUTIONAL TRANSITION

Transitions that occur when institutional leadership changes—i.e., the school gets a new president, provost, dean, and or vice president (VP) for advancement—can result in challenges that make it much harder for members of an A Team to do their jobs. Sometimes these challenges occur because of the period of transition itself: Either a position is left unfilled temporarily, and people are hesitant to make a final decision "before the new boss arrives," or it's filled by someone on an interim basis who is reluctant to embark on a plan that may simply be canceled later.

At other times, the challenge occurs because the new administrator faces a steep learning curve and, while gaining experience through trial and error, makes so many errors that it becomes a trial for everyone else. At still other times, the new administrator turns out to be more F Troop than A Team material and, through fumbling or incompetence, ends up causing more problems than he or she solves.

Leadership changes, particularly when there are a lot of them at once or when the same position is vacated repeatedly, can cause prospective donors to become hesitant about moving forward with a gift because they fear their intent may no longer fit the vision of the new administrative team. Few people would want to endow a chair in ancient philosophy if there's a strong possibility that a new chancellor will reorient the institution's priorities toward engineering and athletics.

Although an experienced A Team can weather this uncertainty, continue to make progress, and provide an element of continuity to the institution, donors often fear there will be a void during periods of leadership transition and hold off on making large commitments until the new administrator's priorities become clear. An important role that the A Team can play during this time is thus to assure donors and prospective donors that the fundamental mission and vision of the institution won't change, that you will be completely transparent about the new administrator's plans as soon as they are made public, and that you will serve as a liaison to help the new leadership team understand what the concerns of donors are and how they might be addressed.

None of this advice may seem very helpful, however, when you have that sinking feeling that the new administrative team just might be an F Troop. If you've never worked for a boss you considered incompetent or, even worse, capable of causing lasting harm to the institution, consider yourself lucky. Inept supervisors occur in all professions, and higher education is no exception. Sooner or later most of us find ourselves working for the type of boss that might be called a *Commander Queeg*, after the character from Herman Wouk's novel *The Caine Mutiny* (1952).

In Wouk's novel, Lieutenant Commander Philip Francis Queeg is assigned to a minesweeper, the U.S.S. Caine, in the Pacific theater during World War II and quickly becomes a textbook example of an incompetent leader entrusted with responsibilities too great for him to handle. He blames others for his failures, is emotionally unstable, can be cowardly, spends most of his time in his own quarters, bullies others, acts despotically, and may well be psychopathic. Queeg fails so completely at his assignment that he risks losing the Caine by charting the wrong course in the midst of a typhoon. Lieutenant Stephen Maryk invokes section 184 of the Navy manual to have Queeg declared mentally unfit for duty, seizes command of the ship, and proceeds to steer it to safety. For his actions, Maryk is then court-martialed, but Queeg's neurotic behavior is clearly demonstrated during the trial, and Maryk is acquitted. Nevertheless, once the trial is over, Maryk's own lawyer reveals that, although he had successfully defended his client, he regarded Queeg as the one who had been treated unjustly: The duty of a subordinate, the lawyer says, is always to assist a senior officer, not to undermine him, and Maryk's actions were potentially far more damaging than were Queeg's. At the end of the novel, in a letter written by Willie Keith, one of the junior officers who served alongside Maryk, this surprising position is explained:

> I don't think Maryk had to relieve the captain. Either Queeg would have come north by himself when things got bad enough, or Maryk would have done it and Queeg would have strung along after some beefing and there would have been no damned court-martial. And the Caine would have stayed in action instead of holing up in San Francisco during the biggest actions of the war. The idea is, once you get an incompetent ass of a skipper—and it's a chance of war—there's nothing to do but serve him as though he were the wisest and the best, cover his mistakes, keep the ship going, and bear up. (Wouk, 1952, 468)

That unexpected conclusion was striking enough that William H. Whyte, Jr. used it as his central example of "the organization man" mentality of the 1950s, characterizing it as

> an astounding denial of individual responsibility. The system is presented as having such a mystique that apparent evil becomes a kind of good. ... We are asked to accept the implied moral that it would have been better to let the ship and several hundred men perish rather than question authority. (Whyte, 1957, 271–272).

Those two positions, Wouk's and Whyte's, will interest anyone who has worked at a college or university long enough to serve under one or more Commander Queegs. To be sure, the incompetence or tyranny of an administrator is highly unlikely to result in the death of one's coworkers, but many of us have encountered a supervisor who seems bent on a course of action that will alienate a valued donor, drive away potential students, cause funding to be diverted from more important projects, lead to a lawsuit or a major grievance, or result in some other type of serious, perhaps even irreparable harm.

For this reason, the question that members of an A Team must sometimes ask themselves is, *What is the appropriate action to take when your disagreement with the boss is, not merely occasional or the result of a somewhat different perspective, but significant, ongoing, and possibly destructive?* The team members can follow Maryk's course and "mutiny," adopt Willie Keith's approach and support the supervisor regardless of any misgivings, seek to undermine the boss behind the scenes, provide the best advice he or she can and hope that reason will prevail, resign his or her position, or take some other course of action. The difficulty comes in knowing which of these approaches is the best in any given situation or whether any of these approaches is preferable in *all* situations.

What members of an A Team decide to do when they no longer have confidence in a member of the upper administration will depend a great deal on the severity of the problem the team is facing and the type of incompetence the supervisor is demonstrating. No one will argue against taking aggressive action in any matter that seriously threatens someone's life or safety, as well as in cases where irreversible damage could be done to the institution.

Yet most of the situations an A Team faces don't reach this level of crisis, no matter how important they may seem at the time. In the vast majority of cases, it's far better for people to provide their best advice constructively in private, make as compelling a case as possible for the course of action they are recommending, and abide by their supervisor's decision even if they don't like it. In other words, as unpalatable as we may find the conclusion of Wouk's novel, there are many times in which he's actually right. An A Team can do greater harm than its leader if its members do any of the following:

- *They speak poorly about the supervisor to others.* It's natural in all situations to vent to our friends and colleagues about those who are in authority over us. Students complain about professors, professors complain about chairs, chairs complain about deans, and deans complain about the provost and president. As long as that kind of normal griping doesn't get out of hand, it's benign and probably even somewhat beneficial since it can help to relieve tensions.

   But badmouthing the boss in a manner that is intense, bitter, severe, and routine is never appropriate. First, it doesn't make the boss look bad; it makes *us* look disloyal. Those who hear our remarks will soon lose sympathy for our repeated complaints and begin to develop some understanding of our supervisor.

Second, that time of backbiting sets a bad precedent. It conveys the message that we regard it as acceptable to demonstrate overt disrespect behind the supervisor's back. That lesson isn't one we want to convey to those who report to us.

Third, it can hurt us by being reported to others. Inevitably people talk and, in an academic setting, we can't expect that what we say won't be reported to our boss by someone. As soon as that happens, our relationship with the boss changes irreparably. At best, our work will now be more difficult. At worst, we could find ourselves looking for new employment opportunities.

- *They attempt to undermine a decision that's been made.* One of the most hypocritical actions any member of an A Team can take is to agree with a decision in public, but work behind the scenes to sabotage the plan his or her boss has made. This approach doesn't just *look* disloyal; it *is* disloyal, and it suggests that the employee can no longer be trusted in any of his or her statements and actions. As we say repeatedly throughout this book, a great deal of our effectiveness as members of an A Team is a product of our credibility. As soon as our credibility is lost, the opportunity we have to serve our institutions and coworkers is severely diminished.

  It's a failure of leadership to tell our supervisors that we support an action but to do little to make that action successful. If we've expressed reservations about a particular course of action but were outvoted, our job then becomes to make sure the plan has a fair chance to succeed in spite of our misgivings. Anything short of this committed effort makes the problem our own, not our boss's.

- *They make it clear to others that they were the ones who advised against a strategy if it doesn't work out.* No one likes to hear "I told you so." Pointing out to others that we were right and our supervisor was wrong serves very little purpose. It makes us seem petty, strains our relationship with our supervisor, and doesn't change the outcome anyway.

  While we may think we appear prescient when we have an opportunity to point out we'd been right all along, we're more likely to discover that other people's recollections don't match our own and that the boss isn't grateful for being reminded of his or her error. Members of an A Team are discreet. They're team players. So, they may take some inner satisfaction in being right, but they keep it to themselves.

It's always possible, of course, that, in your own situation, you serve under someone as unstable and dangerous as Wouk's Commander Queeg and that it's your duty as a professional to go over that person's head and report the matter to the governing board. These situations do occur, but we must remember that they're extremely rare. A member of an A Team should be fully convinced that the damage that will be caused by his or her supervisor will be egregious enough to warrant such radical action, and then must be willing to take the consequences for his or her decision.

If you find yourself confronted with situations like this more than once in your career, it's far more likely that it's *your* judgments that are questionable than that one of your supervisors after another has been incompetent. In fact, it may be time to reflect on whether the people who report to you aren't really the ones who are serving under their own Commander Queeg.

EXTENDED INTERIM LEADERSHIP

One of the authors' close friends works at a university with a longstanding focus on the STEM disciplines (science, technology, engineering, and math). In a conversation, we asked him whether his school was developing any new programs at the moment. He reflected a bit and then said, "Well, we seem to be bent on becoming national leaders in the field of acting."

"Acting?" we asked in surprise. "How does that fit in with your school's mission?"

"I'm not sure," he replied. "But it must be true. Right now we have an acting president, an acting provost, four acting deans, and twenty-three acting department chairs."

A large number of people in temporary positions, like those described by our friend, triggers anxiety both inside and outside the institution. Students worry whether their programs will be eliminated before they graduate. Faculty members fear for their jobs. Staff members worry that they'll be transferred to a different unit where the workload might be greater and their colleagues less agreeable. And donors worry that the initiatives they start today may be ignored tomorrow, causing their generosity to be wasted.

While most people understand that progress requires constant tweaking and periodic substantive change, they may still be afraid that new leadership will introduce an entirely new direction and focus to the institution. They wonder whether the resulting "new world order" will still have a place for them. Even if it does, will that place still be as satisfying as the one they occupy now?

To help provide stability in a time of transition, many schools will appoint temporary leaders to help bridge the passage from the old to the new. Although the terms *interim* and *acting* are often used interchangeably, there actually is an important difference between being, say, an acting president and an interim president.

- People in *acting* roles have authority *delegated* to them. Often when an administrator is out for a few days of medical leave or vacation, another person will be assigned that person's responsibilities in an acting capacity. An *acting* president, VP, provost, or dean is thus usually not expected to launch any new initiatives.

To a large extent, administrators in an acting capacity are expected merely to maintain their offices' day-to-day functions and to be available in case a decision is needed during an emergency.

- People in *interim* roles have the full authority and responsibility of a position, but only for a set period. Interim administrators are often appointed while searches are under way to fill the position they're holding temporarily. An *interim* president, VP, provost, or dean may well launch certain initiatives as a means of continuing progress until a permanent replacement can be found.

Of course, there is really no such thing as a *permanent* replacement, merely someone with an *open-ended* as opposed to a *term* contract. In the end, everyone moves out of a position in order to step down, accept another job, retire, or something similar.

One advantage of interim positions is that they provide a clear separation between the terms of the former administrator and the new, permanent replacement. That separation allows the new administrator to be his or her own person and not continually have his or her actions compared to what the former president, VP, provost, or dean would have done.

In general, acting or interim administrators should be excellent managers and possibly good leaders, while permanent administrators should excel at both leadership and management. They should have personalities that convey a sense of calm continuity, since certain internal and external stakeholders will need reassurance that everything they value won't be lost during this period of leadership transition.

CASE STUDY #1

The authors witnessed a classic example of how extended interim leadership can be detrimental at a medium-sized university that had four presidents within six years. Even presidents who were supposed to be permanent came and left during that time as they received more attractive job offers or proved to be a poor fit for the institution. That rapid turnover left the advancement division of the university without a clear directive as to what its priorities should be for fundraising and community engagement.

What appeared to be a plan would be developed only to be abandoned a month or two later as new interim VPs were appointed by the presidents and then replaced when a new president appeared. When the last of the four presidents was hired, a decision was finally made to begin a national search for a strong and experienced leader who could bring a lasting vision to the school's fundraising efforts. In the meantime, yet another interim VP for advancement was appointed to carry on the day-to-day operations of the unit. This new supervisor was a member of the staff with no real experience in development activities who had risen through the ranks largely by always being available to fill in wherever someone was needed. The result struck many development officers (DOs) and academic administrators at the institution as an illustration of the well-known *Peter Principle*: the theory that people rise in any organizational hierarchy until they reach their level of incompetence (see Peter and Hull, 1969).

The new acting VP was abrasive, reluctant to consider the ideas of anyone other than those on the president's executive staff (none of whom had any development experience either), and widely disliked by the faculty and staff. The president, being new to the university, hadn't witnessed the damage this person had done while in previous roles. The president also didn't understand how the development staff would regard this appointment as a punishment or repudiation of the work they'd been doing through a very tumultuous period.

The new acting VP entered the role with a philosophy that no major decisions would be made until a permanent VP for development was found. The division was thus encouraged to "tread water"—keep raising small gifts for the annual fund and performing any background work requested by the executive team while refraining from new initiatives or the pursuit of new gifts until a new VP and strategic plan were in place—for a period that could last as long as two years. Searches to replace several development and communication officers who had retired were abandoned. Their positions went unfilled. And their responsibilities were redistributed to a smaller and now demoralized advancement team.

As time went on, the development staff saw its acting VP grow increasingly confident in this leadership role and willing to make decisions further and further outside this person's field of expertise. Moreover, as a member of the executive staff, the acting VP funneled all information about development to the president, often with a spin that the staff wasn't performing its tasks properly and that there was active resistance to the president's plans for the future.

As a strong believer in policies and systems, the acting VP also developed a number of new committees and procedures that slowed down the pace of work throughout the division and extended the time it took to get a decision on even relatively minor issues. One of these new committees was a Tangible Gifts Committee that would consider all requests for the university to accept non-cash contributions, evaluate their cost-benefit ratio, and recommend when the institution should accept, modify, or reject the proposal.

In order to have experts in many different fields on the committee, the members were largely chosen from across the faculty, and any discipline that wanted representation was allowed to nominate at least one member. The acting VP personally selected the members who would serve on the committee and charged them to consider, not merely the value of each gift it was asked to review, but such factors as its maintenance, space requirements, and suitability to the university's mission.

An elderly couple in the area had amassed a large collection of musical instruments, some of which dated back to the early Renaissance. Their relatives weren't interested in the collection, and so the couple was looking for an institution that would preserve it intact for its immense historical value. Several years earlier, the couple had approached the university about accepting the collection for display either in the library or in the music department and, under a previous interim president, a gift agreement had been approved by the university's legal counsel. Since the collection would come to the institution as part of a bequest, finalizing the agreement was not considered to be urgent, and the documentation remained in the division of advancement until the acting VP was appointed.

Unexpectedly, however, the couple who wanted to make the gift developed some health problems. The wife fell ill in another state, and the prognosis didn't look good. The couple was thus in a hurry to get its affairs in order and pressed the university for the gift agreement so that it could be signed and detailed plans for the bequest be made. The acting VP concluded that the proposed gift was perfectly suited to the charge of the Tangible Gifts Committee and asked it to review the document before it would be presented to the couple.

There was a problem, however. The wife's illness had occurred in the spring and, by the time the VP sent the matter to the committee, it was already mid-May. Since nearly all the members of the Tangible Gifts Committee served on the faculty, they were no longer under contract until late August. The university was unionized, and the collective bargaining agreement in force forbade the administration from assigning the faculty any service responsibilities during periods for which the faculty was not being paid.

As a result, the chair of the committee wrote back to the acting VP that the Tangible Gifts Committee would be happy to begin reviewing the proposed gift agreement—in about three or four months, once the fall semester was under way. The chair also noted that, since it hadn't yet developed guidelines for a tangible gifts review process that could be uniformly applied across the university, it could even be late in the next academic year before the gift agreement would receive full consideration. Then, if changes were recommended, additional time might be required.

The acting VP considered that timetable reasonable and decided that, in the meantime, it would be useful for the institution to request several third-party quotes from professional appraisers to determine the value of items and the cost that would be entailed in their storage and maintenance.

When the matter was discussed at a meeting of the president's cabinet, another VP speculated that the cost to move, maintain, and house the instruments could easily exceed a million dollars. The cabinet thus encouraged the acting VP to have the DO involved in the gift go back to the couple and inform them that, in order for the gift to be considered, the donors would have to accompany the tangible property with a cash gift of $1.2 million so that the university wouldn't incur any cost for "helping the couple dispose of this property."

The DO reluctantly presented this information to the couple, who were understandably outraged both by the amount of the request ("the university's attempt at extortion," as the husband put it) and its willingness to reconsider a gift agreement that the donors had considered already finalized.

Negotiations and recriminations went back and forth for the next year, with the couple finally agreeing that the university could sell some of the instruments up to a maximum of $500,000 in order to pay for the moving and upkeep of the others. Even so, the acting VP remained hesitant to approve the revised gift agreement. "I'm not an expert in historical musical instruments," the acting VP said. "And I certainly don't want to be saddled with having to sell some of them. Let's wait until we get another set of appraisals—those we did earlier are now nearly a year out of date, and the market may have changed—and the Tangible Gifts Committee still hasn't finished its work on what our uniform policy will be. I don't see the need for a rush here. The instruments won't be any less historic if we take our time and do this right."

This might be the sort of thing we want to defer until we get a permanent VP for advancement in place."

About a month after the DO heard these words from the acting VP, the couple's health deteriorated even further. The wife died, and the husband was moved to an assisted living center. Since no gift agreement was signed, the husband offered the instruments to a museum about a hundred miles from the university, and the museum accepted them immediately.

In the news story that appeared about the museum's new collection, it was announced that the value of the gift had been appraised at over fifty million dollars. The museum was confident that, by partnering with a local college and a society for the arts to promote the exhibit, increased ticket sales would pay for all the expenses required to move, insure, and maintain the instruments in less than a month.

Question: Could an A Team have done anything differently in this situation so as to achieve a better outcome for the donors and the university alike?

Case Study Discussion

This case study illustrates what can happen when several different challenges combine to create a truly severe problem:

- First, the high administrative turnover at the institution left it without a clear vision for the future and a plan for achieving it.
- Second, the extended time that administrators were kept in interim roles slowed decision-making at the university even further, resulting in alienation of donors and a poor public image for the university.
- Third, the acting VP appears to be an F Troop personality: incapable of doing the job, unjustifiably confident about his or her abilities as a leader, hampered by poor interpersonal skills, and unwilling to consider advice from people who had a great deal of experience in their jobs.

In an environment so filled with landmines, it's uncertain whether even an A Team could lead this process to a successful conclusion. If there is any hope of success, however, it would come from taking full advantage of the team approach to fundraising and by demonstrating a level of leadership at the middle of the institution that was not in evidence at its highest levels. Here's one possibility.

The acting VP seems to trust the importance of hierarchy (thus having confidence in the decisions of the president's cabinet while remaining suspicious of the motives of others) and faculty expertise (thus creating a Tangible Gifts Committee that consists largely of faculty members). An A Team could use that insight to try to move the process along. Instead of having requests come from the team's development staff, communications could flow from the most senior academic member of the team.

For example, the dean of the College of Liberal and Creative Arts, the unit in which the music department is housed, could draft an email message to the chair of the Tangible Gifts Committee, with copies sent to the acting VP of advancement as well as the provost (the dean's direct supervisor), that says something like the following:

Dear Taylor and Members of the Tangible Gifts Committee,

I wonder if you could help me with a problem I'm trying to solve. As you know, for about two years, there has been discussion about an exceptional collection of historical musical instruments that two valued friends of the college wish to bequest to the university. More than a year ago, the university presented a fully approved gift agreement to the prospective donors. But due to the critically ill health of one of the donors and our own administrative changes, the matter was not finalized at that time.

In the intervening year, with the formation of the university's Tangible Gift Committee, the gift agreement has been revisited in light of certain expenses associated with maintaining this collection, and some have even questioned the university's desire to accept the gift at all. Through our further contact with the donors, they have agreed to allow several pieces to be sold through a third-party representative so as to provide the funds needed for the associated costs of the relocation, installation, insurance and maintenance of this important collection.

The donors are very eager to have this agreement settled, not only for themselves, but for their daughter who will be the executor of their estate. She is in agreement with all the actions and plans that have been made to date. I, too, am eager to have this agreement settled since I believe the gift will be a valuable asset for students of the College of Liberal and Creative Arts and other members of the university community as a whole. The gift aligns well with the president's initiative to enhance community engagement and has the potential to bring numerous visitors (some of whom are likely to become new donors) to campus.

It's my professional judgment that accepting this gift in a timely manner will enhance our campus, coursework, and environment becoming, in its own way, as much a selling point for the university to students of the arts and humanities as our beautiful new hockey arena is for those with a strong interest in athletics.

For this reason, I'm respectfully requesting the Tangible Gift Committee to recommend to the university's leadership team that the donors' collection be accepted at this time so that a revised gift agreement can be fully executed so as to seal this commitment. This collection will add significant value to our university's tangible assets, and I fully support its acquisition.

Thank you so much for considering this request.

Sincerely,
[NAME], Dean
College of Liberal and Creative Arts

This message could be effective on a variety of different levels. First, it gives a voice of academic authority to the request that the DO, working alone, wouldn't have.

Second, it provides a rationale for accepting the gift: The dean doesn't want the musical instruments simply because they're being offered but because they would relate well to the educational and research mission of the college.

Third, it ties acceptance of the gift—gently but clearly—to the president's strategic vision; while not exactly saying, "You don't want to be the one who stands in the way of the president's plan for community engagement, do you?" it sends that message implicitly.

Fourth, it clears away any objections people might have, such as "What do the donors' heirs think about this idea? What is the university's advantage in accepting the gift? How will we pay for the gift's relocation, installation, insurance and maintenance?"

Fifth, and perhaps most importantly, it gives the acting VP someone to blame if things go wrong. "Look," we can imagine the acting VP saying, "I never wanted to accept this gift in the first place. But the dean said it was a good idea, so ..."

That last observation provides the A Team with a useful tool in dealing with any members of an F Troop that it may happen to encounter. Many times an F Troop either acts very slowly or does nothing at all because it's afraid of being blamed for doing something wrong. *If an A Team demonstrates that it's willing to accept the consequences if a plan goes awry, it eliminates one of the F Troop's primary motivations for inactivity.* Provide an F Troop with shelter from a possible storm, and it will almost always flee to safety, thus getting out of your way.

CHALLENGES CAUSED BY COMPETITION
WITHIN INSTITUTIONAL LEADERSHIP

Another common feature of F Troops is that they engage in negative, not positive competition. Make no mistake about it: A Teams are highly competitive. They are motivated by their desire to have the highest contribution rates among all the other development groups at their institutions. But they'd never undermine another group, poach its donors, or turn down an opportunity to help the institution just because someone else might get credit for it.

That type of behavior is more typical of an F Troop, and it's encountered more often than you might expect even in the non-profit world where ethical principles are supposed to be guiding the staff's behavior. Competition often occurs between the provost and the VP for research and between the VP for development and the VP for business affairs. That competition is positive when it's focused on better ways of educating students, conducting research, and producing better results with greater efficiency. But it's destructive when it's focused on building one's own résumé or simply one-upping a presumed rival. A case study that the authors once observed illustrates the damage this type of competition can create.

CASE STUDY #2

For historical reasons that had to do with purchasing the facilities of a now-defunct local academy, Snooty Hills College has long had two degree-completion programs for adult returning students: a fairly traditional program on its main campus in Scholar's Grove and a more experimental program on its branch campus in Far Provinces. Each program has its own director, and each has a claim for distinction. The director of the more traditional degree-completion program often cites that program's exceptional rigor and the fact that "We don't cut any corners. The adult students who complete their degrees here in Scholar's Grove meet the same standards as our residential students. They're in class for the same hours, write the same number of papers, and take the same tests."

The director of the experimental program sees the matter differently. "We recognize that adult students have different needs than traditional college-aged students do. They have full-time jobs, are often taking care of children (and perhaps aging parents), and may have been away from school for many years. That's why our tutorials and online classes work so well for adult students who were seeking to complete degrees they'd begun years earlier: We meet them wherever they are and take them where they want to go."

In different circumstances that level of competition may have been friendly and beneficial to the students of Snooty Hills. But each director wanted sole responsibility for both programs and was hoping to achieve an even higher administrative role. As a result, they found it hard to work together and even to be in the same room with one another. Each claimed ownership of Snooty Hills' "only real" degree-completion program and spoke disparagingly of the other to anyone who would listen.

The person who suffered the most from this poor relationship was the sole DO assigned to both programs. For years now, external support for these programs had been minimal, mostly a few small gifts that alumni gave, restricting their gift to the program they attended. These funds amounted to little more than a small supplemental account that the directors relied on when their supply funds were running low.

Recently, Snooty Hills College was approached by the Wealthy Magnanimous Foundation (WMF), an organization committed to excellence in adult degree-completion programs. WMF wanted to purchase naming rights to Snooty Hills' programs for $25 million. In a similar way to how it interacted with other such programs, WMF wouldn't administer the program or control its curriculum. It simply wanted its name attached to successful programs and the opportunity to involve administrators of these programs in an annual conference that encouraged colleges and universities to learn from one another and adopt best practices for serving this important segment of the student population.

The director of the program at Far Provinces immediately expressed enthusiasm for this idea. A $25 million endowment would generate a million dollars a year. Split evenly between the two programs, that funding could help them eliminate some deferred maintenance over time, update their technology, and greatly increase their scholarship funding.

Perhaps because of the strong support for the idea by the director at Far Provinces, the director at the Scholar's Grove location expressed no interest at all in this award. "I'm very familiar with the work of the Wealthy Magnanimous Foundation," this director said. "And I don't trust them. They say they won't be involved in internal decisions but, once you accept their money, they try to put their stamp on everything: programming, staffing, facilities—the works. I want nothing to do with them."

That claim disturbed the college's executive team so much that the VP for development called each of the other schools that had accepted WMF funding. No one would confirm the negative impression that the director at Scholar's Grove had of the foundation. Even more interesting, the VP learned that the grant offered to Snooty Hills College was far larger than that received by any other school. When this information became public, the director at Scholar's Grove said, "That doesn't change a thing. WMF has always been a problem, and the people there are terrible to work with. This deal is terrible, and we need to turn it down."

The college then contacted the WMF and inquired into the possibility of having the organization purchase only the naming rights to the program on the Far Provinces campus. WMF said that it wasn't interested; its sole reason for making this offer was to get its name associated with long-established adult degree-completion programs, and that wouldn't happen unless it was involved with both of the programs at Snooty Hills.

That message was then conveyed to the director at Scholar's Grove who replied, "Look, if I'm going to be forced to do this, then I want all the money. That's my final position: Change the name of both programs if you like, but Scholar's Grove gets access to the entire $25 million."

When that declaration was reported to the executive team, the president decided that enough was enough. Both directors were called in, as well as the DO responsible for the two programs and the institution's senior staff. The president declared in no uncertain terms that the college *would* accept the grant from the WMF, both programs *would* bear the WMF name, and the two directors *would* work out their differences.

With no real advice on *how* they were to work out their differences, the president left to attend another meeting, and the two directors each began to stake out their positions, becoming more and more intransigent as the afternoon wore on.

In the weeks that followed, the DO tried to meet the president's requirements. The director at Far Provinces complied with all the DO's requests for information, providing enrollment figures, graduation rates, projections for the next five years, and other key pieces of information that the WMF had asked for. The director at Scholar's Grove provided information only grudgingly—usually in an incomplete or poorly written manner—and claimed that the DO's instructions were either unclear or continually changing.

In addition, the director at Scholar's Grove kept disparaging the WMF and ultimately managed to persuade most of the staff members that the grant was a terrible idea. The process dragged on for another year, and the WMF grew increasingly impatient for Snooty Hills' final application for the grant. The director at Scholar's Grove stopped all external fundraising, claiming that the excessive demands for information were putting a strain on the staff and leaving no time for any development activities. Moreover, "Nobody's going to give us money anyway because we're going to be associated with that WMF name." (The director at Far Provinces raised $600,000 in external funding during this period.)

As the second full year of the project drew to a close, the executive VP of the WMF sent a letter to the president of Snooty Hills College, stating that it was clear the institution wasn't committed to a partnership with WMF and so the organization was rescinding its offer for funding.

Question: Could an A Team have done anything differently in this situation so as to achieve a better outcome for the college?

Case Study Discussion

Certain types of conflicts are inevitable and, when it comes to turf wars like this one, it's unclear whether even an A Team could solve a problem of this magnitude. But one advantage of the team approach is that the opportunity to find a workable solution doesn't fall on only one person's shoulders. In the case summarized above, the DO felt trapped because of the obligation to serve the directors of both programs.

As the New Testament passage suggests, "No one can serve two masters. Either you will hate the one and love the other, or you will be devoted to the one and despise the other" (Matthew 6:24 and Luke 16:13). No one would fault this DO for feeling greater sympathy (and thus working harder) for the director on the Far Provinces campus who provided information in a timely manner and generally made the DO's job easier.

But with both directors acting in some ways as the DO's supervisor, it's difficult for the DO to take too aggressive a tone with the director on the Scholar's Grove campus and insist that a more cooperative tone be adopted so that the grant application can be submitted.

If an A Team were involved, there is a greater chance that someone in the group could be regarded by both directors as an honest broker to resolve these differences. It's also possible that the academic officer (AO) on the team could be an effective voice to the president and provost about what the problems were during the process, who was ignoring the president's injunction to work out the disagreement, and how the matter might be handled more effectively.

It's certainly easier to imagine a more positive outcome to this scenario—perhaps a reassignment of the Scholar's Grove director to other duties and a subsequent submission of the grant application in a more timely manner—with an A Team involved than with isolated individuals trying to address the problem.

One factor complicating this story is the role of the provost. Since both directors were in charge of academic programs, the provost is a logical candidate for the administrator who would work out a resolution to the impasse that resulted and, if necessary, override the decisions (or lack thereof) of one or both of the directors.

But there's no indication in the case study that the provost demonstrated this type of leadership. As a result, the president had to intervene, and, although a direct order was given that the two directors should come to a resolution, the lack of follow-through by the president caused the problem to continue unsolved. That situation, too, might have been avoided if an A Team had been involved and at least one of its members updated the president and provost about the need for a swift resolution despite the reluctance of one director to see the matter through.

With a team approach, various members of the group can help compensate for the absence of strong leadership in the upper administration. Deans, department chairs, and even individual faculty can sometimes serve as the "face" of a program when a president or provost is too busy (or not sufficiently interested) to serve in that role.

At the same time, members of the advancement staff can use their familiarity with investment strategies and alternative ways to package philanthropy to continue the conversation with prospective donors if a conversation seems stalled on the academic side of the institution. Advisory boards and governing boards may also be able to assist. The key in each case is to make use of all the human resources available and not allow one individual to bear full responsibility for moving a project forward.

CHALLENGES CAUSED BY INEXPERIENCE

Fundraising, like enrollment management and leading an honors program, tends to be one of those activities that many administrators assume they know all about—even if they have no experience or training in this area. On the other side of the institution, many fundraisers assume that, because they do have experience soliciting gifts, they know most of what they need to know about *academic* fundraising.

Both of these assumptions are false, and mistakes caused by inexperience can cause lasting damage to a program. F Troops believe they know everything they need to know about a new area; A Teams study and gain experience before venturing into uncharted territory.

The challenges that arise from an administrator's inexperience often occur when a new president or chancellor arrives on the scene, particularly if the successful candidate is someone who's never headed an institution before. New presidents often want to work alongside their own team.

For this reason, shortly after a new president has been hired, it's common for institutions to find themselves with many new VPs, several new deans and directors, and a number of new people in various support roles. The result is that many employees are in new roles simultaneously, with at least some of them unfamiliar with that specific assignment or the responsibilities at that level of the institution. When it comes to development activities, that level of inexperience can cause serious problems.

In a report prepared by the Council of Independent Colleges (CIC), Harold Hartley and Eric Godin note that only 40% of first-time presidents at American universities ever served as provosts, while 23% had been administrators in a non-academic area of a college or university.

Within the CIC itself (an organization that represents about five hundred small and mid-sized, independent, liberal arts colleges and universities), only

35% of new presidents had previous experience as provosts and 33% had been non-AOs. Even more striking, a full 13% of new CIC presidents came to their positions from outside higher education, and only 22% were hired internally at the same institution where they had worked in another capacity (report available at www.cic.edu/Research-and-Data/Research-Studies/Documents/CICPresSurvey.pdf).

What these figures mean is that a lot of institutions are being headed by chief executive officers who have only limited experience with the organizational culture of colleges, universities, and community colleges. But working with college professors is different from working with other kinds of employees. They are all experts in their fields, hold advanced degrees, and view themselves more as independent contractors than as traditional employees. As a result, even those presidents who *have* worked in higher education, but come from such areas as the division of business affairs or community relations, often find themselves ill prepared for success in their new roles.

In a study conducted by Robert L. Jackson, the president of Murray State University in Kentucky, it was revealed that, even though most public university presidents don't have a strong fundraising background, they spend roughly *seven days per month* in fundraising activities. About a fifth of the presidents who participated in the study meet or talk with their chief DOs *daily*. Almost 70% said they interacted with their chief DOs two or three times each week. A total of 37% of presidents said that fundraising ranked number one or two among their most important duties, and nearly three-quarters included fundraising among their top three responsibilities (report available at digitalcommons.wku.edu/cgi/viewcontent.cgi?article=1008&context=ijlc).

Similar results were reported in a 2013 study conducted by *The Chronicle of Higher Education*. In a survey of 400 college and university presidents, respondents ranked "meeting fundraising goals" as fifth (tied with having a good working relationship with the governing board and improving the quality of educational programs) on a list of eighteen measures of success for chief executive officers in higher education. Even more strikingly, fundraising was ranked first in importance when the presidents were asked to prioritize strategies for lowering costs for students (report available at: www.maguireassoc.com/wp-content/uploads/Chronicle-Presidents-Survey-for-Education-Counsel.pdf).

This disconnect between the type of experience new presidents bring to their positions and the activities they need to perform once on the job illustrates one of the problems that faces many institutions of higher education today. Perhaps the impact those problems can have will be even clearer after we explore another case study.

CASE STUDY #3

No one could argue that the new president was unfamiliar with the college. She'd received her bachelor's degree there thirty years earlier and had always credited the school with launching her on her very successful academic career. Upon her arrival, she was sure that she could help reinvigorate an institution that had grown stodgy over the years. Enrollment was steady, but certainly not growing. Contributions to the annual fund had stagnated. And the school's endowment was, by the president's estimation, roughly a third of what a school of that size should have.

In assembling a new leadership team, she replaced the provost, VP for development, and VP for enrollment management with people she thought might introduce "fresh new ideas" from outside the institution. She asked the VP for business affairs and the VP for community relations to step down, too, replacing them both with their associate VPs who had been hired only the year before.

Since the president had never had executive-level experience before (she had been VP for strategic planning at a midsized regional university), she was particularly eager that her chief DO have a strong enough portfolio to help her move the institution forward. She was fortunate, therefore, in hiring a VP for development who had been a former state cabinet member as Secretary of Commerce for four years and who received the unanimous recommendation of the school's board of trustees.

Although never a member of the faculty or staff of any college, the new VP worked his way up through a number of state offices, earned a bachelor's degree in political science as well as an MBA, and seemed to know everyone in state and local government.

Success seemed to come almost immediately. The new VP contacted another former public official who had gone on to make a fortune in the financial services industry, and persuaded her to offer a gift large enough to buy the naming rights to the college's women's studies program. Back in his days as Secretary of Commerce, the VP had heard a few vague, unsubstantiated stories about some questionable deals the donor had made for her client. But he knew that rumors often attach themselves to successful people because others are envious of them and gave the matter no further thought. The gift for several million dollars was accepted, booked, and an official naming ceremony was scheduled for the women's studies program.

The chair of the department of women's studies had previously worked successfully as part of an A Team that had also included the DO of the College of Social Programs. These two staff members were then paired again to perform the background work in preparation for the naming ceremony.

Almost immediately after they began performing their due diligence, however, the team began to discover that the stories of financial improprieties were not merely rumors. Charges had been filed, although the matter was later dropped after the donor made a settlement with her accusers for an undisclosed sum. Even worse, there had been serious allegations of sexual misconduct in return for insider trading information, parties at which illegal drugs had been consumed, and investments in a broad range of industries with questionable records of human rights.

Any one of these issues could bring the college a great deal of negative publicity. If all the stories came out together, the result would be an utter disaster.

The team brought their findings to the VP for development. To their surprise, he told them that, since there hadn't been any convictions resulting from the charges and since all private suits had been dropped, the university should continue with its plans to accept the gift. The members of the A Team disagreed and requested a meeting with the president. Reluctantly, the VP agreed.

At that meeting, the team members presented their findings, and then the VP for development presented her argument for accepting the gift as planned. The A Team told the president that there was cause to question the donor's intent:

- Was the donor using the gift to garner good will from the public in case the allegations of misconduct once again became a serious issue in the media?
- If even some of the allegations were true, what could the repercussions be for the university?
- Why, since the donor had never before been involved in philanthropy, had this gift been offered now?

The president listened to both sides carefully and then announced her decision. She felt that she needed to trust the judgment of her new executive team and so agreed to proceed with accepting the gift and scheduling the naming ceremony.

On the day of the event, the headline in the local newspaper was, "College Names Program for Accused Racketeer," and television stations throughout the region ran stories about all the other scandals surrounding the donor. Although the school's public relations office did its best to recapture the narrative of the story, the damage had already been done. Other donors called the school to cancel their pledges, and a large number of prospective students withdrew their applications.

Within a week, there was so much negative publicity that the school felt compelled to refuse acceptance of the donation. Despite these efforts, however, the institution found that it was still trying to repair its damaged reputation more than five years later.

Question: Could the A Team have done anything more to avoid this outcome?

Case Study Discussion

Regardless of how different the organizational culture of higher education is from the corporate world; at a certain point your boss is still your boss. The truly difficult challenge posed by this particular case is that two levels of the A Team's supervisors—both the president and VP—are embarking on a clearly ill-advised course of action because of their inexperience.

Depending on the relationship that any academic representatives on the team have with the new provost, they may be able to persuade the provost to advocate for a more cautious approach. Even that strategy, however, is fraught with potential problems: The new provost may see his or her loyalties as lying primarily with the president or be reluctant to create conflict with another VP. The team could thus find itself accused of trying to end-run the VP for development and still not have made an effective case that the leadership team finds persuasive. Inexperienced F Troops can only learn certain lessons through experience; in this case, the lesson learned was very expensive.

The crucial element in this case that the team could perhaps have handled differently was the way in which information was presented in the meeting with the president. Since an A Team includes representatives of different divisions of the institution, it could have presented an exceptionally strong case by outlining the effect negative fallout from receipt of the gift could have on each area of the institution.

Rather than speculating on possible scenarios, they also could have researched similar incidents at other colleges and universities as a way of reinforcing that the risks involved in this decision were genuine. In the end, however, the final call rested with the president, and it's uncertain in this scenario whether she would have acted any differently.

CONCLUDING THOUGHTS

The leadership challenges that we explored in this chapter frequently go together. The departure of one president or chancellor can mean that people remain in interim positions for an extended period and, when a new leadership team is finally in place, it may well have a flawed or slow start due to inexperience.

Moreover, the type of inexperience found among those administrators can occur in several different forms. They may be inexperienced in their jobs, as can occur when a politician and not a university insider becomes a university president. They can be inexperienced at their new level of responsibility, as when a dean becomes a provost for the first time. They may be inexperienced at that specific institution, as happens when someone is hired in from another school. And they can be inexperienced in regional culture, as might occur when an administrator from New England is hired to lead an institution in the Deep South.

The worst scenario of all occurs when one or more high-level administrators are inexperienced in all these ways simultaneously. Then you really do have the ingredients for the most destructive type of F Troop imaginable.

Given the importance that fundraising has for leaders in higher education, there's a need for development experience to be featured prominently as a criterion whenever searches are made for high-level administrators. Given the importance of understanding the academic environment for DOs at colleges, universities, and community colleges, there's a need for anyone working in fundraising for higher education to be well grounded in how these institutions work, how faculty members make decisions, and the role that academic administrators play vis-à-vis the faculty in their areas.

Naomi Levine, executive director of the Heyman Center for Philanthropy at New York University, has observed that the education of fundraisers has lagged far behind their career advancement for years. Levine believes that, as fundraising has become more technical and dependent on more advanced knowledge, the training provided to fundraisers should have increased as well (www.contributemedia.com/opinions_details.php?id=1).

That's why programs like those outlined in Appendix II are so important. Credentialed fundraisers are familiar with the history of philanthropy, the psychology of giving, the vehicles through which contributions may be made, the various forms of planned giving, the ethical issue involved in development, trends in philanthropy, current and pending legislation, and ways in which approaches to philanthropy may be affected by gender, age, and ethnicity. Experienced, credentialed fundraisers are well positioned to help an institution achieve its development goals and to avoid costly mistakes while doing so.

REFERENCES

Peter, L. J., & Hull, R. (1969). *The Peter principle*. New York, NY: Bantam.
Whyte, W.H., Jr. (1957). *The organization man*. Garden City, NY: Doubleday.
Wouk, H. (1952). *The Caine mutiny*. Garden City, NY: Doubleday.

RESOURCES

Danner, J., & Coopersmith, M. (2015). *The other "F" word: How smart leaders, teams, and entrepreneurs put failure to work*. Hoboken, NJ: Wiley.
Lencioni, P. M. (2002). *The five dysfunctions of a team: A leadership fable*. San Francisco, CA: Jossey-Bass.

Chapter Three

Using a Team to Pursue Fundraising Strategies

While poor institutional leadership is the most common reason why A Teams sometimes encounter F Troops, it's not the *only* reason. Even experienced, capable administrators sometimes create problems because they pursue development strategies that are ineffective, counterproductive, or less likely to lead to successful results than other measures. Using a team approach can often decrease the probability that an institution's development efforts will stagnate from poor strategy.

On a well-prepared advancement team, at least one member will have advanced training in development activities from a program like those listed in Appendix II. Someone will also be an academic administrator who will have insight into why a particular strategy, which may work extremely well in a corporate environment, will meet resistance from faculty, students, or alumni.

And there will also probably be someone on the team who understands the intricacies of finance and the law so that gift agreements are constructed in a way that best serves the needs of the donor and institution alike. F Troops frequently lack expertise in these areas. They pursue strategies that initially appear easy or that they wrongly believe are transferrable to their institution from a very different kind of college, university, non-profit organization, or business. And the result can be a disaster.

One strategy that F Troops seem particularly enamored with is the single big event: the university gala that's intended to bring in a great deal of revenue during the course of a glamorous evening of food, entertainment, and formal attire. While it may not be the case that every gala is planned and executed by an F Troop, the authors have observed that nearly every F Troop they've experienced seems to love the idea of a gala.

WHY F TROOPS LOVE GALAS

All academic fundraisers commonly use events to increase awareness of their programs and opportunities to network with those who can help them. Throughout an event, employees of the institution can identify, cultivate, and learn more about potential donors. A number of small easily managed events is thus an extremely useful tool in fundraising.

But that tool loses much of its value when a school's executive team wants to secure record-breaking funds through highly ambitious galas. Certainly, a well-timed gala, perhaps as part of a presidential inauguration or to celebrate one of the institution's major anniversaries, can warrant an all-out effort by members of the A Team and result in favorable publicity, a sizable financial gain, and the sense that everyone involved has contributed to a worthwhile effort.

Nevertheless, when galas become annual (or, worse, even more frequent than annual), their value declines precipitously. They are perceived as routine: not a special occasion but one more burden that staff and guests alike are forced to endure. There are diminishing returns when galas are frequent. Each time more and more effort has to be exerted for fewer and fewer results. The galas thus distract academic administrators and development officers (DOs) from other activities that could be of greater benefit to the college or university.

F Troops seem entranced by galas. The idea of a single event resulting in huge financial benefits sounds so appealing. And what kind of event could be easier and more pleasant than one in which all the participants have a chance to dress formally, indulge in lavish forms of food and drink, and dance the night away?

The problem is that galas often don't have a very good cost–benefit ratio. The expenses involved in sponsoring the event are so large that they consume too high a portion of the revenue. Moreover, there's a Catch 22 to sponsoring galas. Many of the potential guests who can afford the high cost of a ticket experience *gala fatigue*: They are solicited for so many events that they grow weary of them or conclude that they're merely being invited because they have the financial resources to attend. They thus feel taken advantage of, and the gala has a negative effect on the school's public image. Particularly in very wealthy communities—such as Scarsdale, the Hamptons, Palm Beach, Malibu, Beverly Hills, and Westport—residents sometimes are invited to several galas each night during "the season" and thus become increasingly discriminating about which events to support.

The broader public often balks at the high ticket prices associated with galas, leaving the institution with a difficult dilemma: Should it reduce the cost of attendance for certain guests (and thus decrease the income generated per ticket even further) or conduct the event with only a relatively small number of guests who pay the full cost (and thus have an event that looks sparsely attended and may not even raise enough income to cover its fixed costs)?

There is fairly clear evidence that you're dealing with an F Troop when a scenario unfolds as follows:

- A successful gala is held as part of a presidential inauguration or significant anniversary.
- The large amount of revenue raised by that event leads administrators to make the gala a regular event.
- At the second or third such gala, ticket sales lag.
- There is an attempt to boost attendance through one or more of the following strategies: tickets become free for members of the faculty and staff; tickets are sold at greatly reduced prices to members of the faculty and staff; units of the institution are allowed to use their own fundraising revenue to purchase tickets for members of the faculty and staff.
- The revenue raised by the gala is either drastically diminished, consists largely of funds simply transferred from one institutional fundraising account to another, or both.
- The level of attendance and revenue generated (at least on paper since much of it involved moving income between development accounts) cause administrators to declare the event a success and to plan another for the following year.

What members of an F Troop often don't realize is that the costs of a gala don't merely include the expenses involved in purchasing food, drink, and entertainment. A gala also has extensive *opportunity costs*: the losses involved in having members of the staff plan and organize such a time-intensive event when their efforts could have been directed toward activities that produce more revenue from a lower overall investment.

A Teams understand that, when people continually propose galas and other large events as opportunities for fundraising, these suggestions are arising from a *failure of imagination*. In this book, we explore many different forms of fundraising—such as skillful cultivation of individual donors and foundations, using volunteer boards to identify prospects, developing affinity travel programs, and the like—that have a much better cost–benefit ratio than galas.

In addition, A Teams are creative enough to formulate their own fundraising strategies over time, tailoring them to the distinctive features of their location, clientele, and institutional mission. They may even pursue ideas that run counter to the "big event thinking" that is common among so many F Troops.

For example, the authors, aware that those living in their service region of Palm Beach tended to experience the very sort of gala fatigue described earlier, developed a fundraising "event" that they called the *Phantom Beach Ball* for which donors contributed $250 each as a joke fee *not to attend yet another gala*. In return, each contributor received a deflated beach ball (a double entendre on the expression *beach ball* meaning both the type of round inflatable toy used at the beach and a lavish, formal dance or cotillion) and a "permission slip" that "excused" the guest from attending the school's fictitious gala (to which tickets were said to cost "a zillion dollars").

The strategy poked gentle fun at the pervasiveness of expensive galas in the region, entailed a cost for the beach ball and associated materials of under a dollar, and at a 1:249 cost–benefit ratio proved far more profitable than a traditional gala. In an Association of Fundraising Professionals 2014 Special Events Report (available for downloading at specialevents. afpfoundation.org/), 40% of the respondents to a survey stated that it cost them between 20 and 99 cents for every dollar raised through galas. An additional 1% revealed that their galas even cost them more than a dollar for each dollar raised!

In a principle advocated by the author and fundraiser James Greenfield, "No event shall be conducted unless the net profit realized will be 50% or more of its gross proceeds" (Greenfield, 1999, 93). Greenfield also defines *successful fiscal management* in fundraising "as achieving net income for a benefit equal to at least 50% of the gross proceeds for the benefit, after excluding contributions and donated materials, in-kind gifts, and so on, from gross income" (Greenfield, 1999, 134).

That's why A Teams conduct a thorough assessment of marketing costs, levels of volunteer engagement, projected attendance, potential sponsors, challenges of scheduling, and the availability of appropriate staff leadership before committing to any large special event. They understand that *complex special events almost always require professional special event planners*.

The Judy Garland/Mickey Rooney trope of "You make the costumes. We'll use my dad's barn. And hey! Let's put on a show!" (see tvtropes.org/pmwiki/ pmwiki.php/Main/HeyLetsPutOnAShow) doesn't work when it comes to academic galas. It's foolish to think that, regardless of how knowledgeable the faculty and staff are about their primary responsibilities, they have the expertise required to pull off highly complex events routinely and at a favorable cost.

CASE STUDY #1

The new vice president (VP) for development at Struggling State University was determined that there wasn't going to be a failure on her watch. Struggling State had hosted four previous black-tie galas with mixed results. For the first event, the idea of a formal dance on the university's newly renovated basketball court seemed novel. It brought back memories of high school dances, attracted a large attendance, and raised enough money that the school could more than double the number of scholarships it was offering.

The second year was still deemed a success, but the amount raised by the event was significantly lower than the previous year and an extraordinary amount of staff time had to be devoted to making the gala seem even more impressive than the one held the previous year. The third and fourth years of the gala weren't profitable at all. Struggling State described them as great triumphs to the local media and cited a large amount of revenue that was gained, but most of the income consisted of regular donors who merely designated what was going to be their annual fund contribution anyway as a contribution made in support of the gala.

BOX 3.1

When you appear to be raising additional funds because of a special project or event, be sure to ask yourself: Are you really raising more money, or are you simply raising the same money you would have raised anyway but now at a different point in the fundraising cycle?

Subtracting the event's actual cost for food, beverages, security, and custodial services plus the hours of staff time that had to be redirected from other fundraising efforts, Struggling State actually lost more than a hundred thousand dollars on each of the galas in those years.

When the VP for advancement was hired, she was charged with turning this situation around and "recapturing the magic" of the first year's gala. She was known for her strong leadership style and convinced that, by cutting waste, using institutional resources for many services that had been outsourced for the first four galas, and setting clear goals for everyone involved, the Fifth Annual Struggling State Basketball Gala would be the university's salvation. It would make her career and position her for recruitment by a more prestigious institution. Viewing failure as not an option, she decided that her best plan for success was as follows:

- Each of the university's fifteen DOs would receive a quota of five hundred full-price tickets.
- Each college or department that had an advisory board would be charged with purchasing or selling at least one ticket per member. Since most members were married, the VP knew that, if even half the members on each board bought a personal ticket and one for a spouse, this target would be easy to reach. This strategy should result in the sale of at least 250 additional tickets.

- Each of the university's ten deans was tasked with purchasing or selling one hundred full price tickets.
- Each of the university's 57 department chairs was given a target of purchasing or selling at least ten full-price tickets.

The deans and department chairs were told that they were first to try to get members of the faculty and staff to pay for the tickets themselves. If that proved to be impossible, the administrators could use their own annual fund accounts to reduce the price of the tickets for members of the faculty and staff or even to provide the tickets for free. With this plan in place, the VP calculated that she was guaranteed sales of at least 9,320 tickets.

Conservatively estimating the number of tickets that would be sold directly to the public by the division of development, the VP confidently predicted that attendance at the gala would reach 10,000: more than four times the attendance of the gala's third and fourth years. At $1,000 a ticket, the gala would gross at least ten million dollars, netting about $7.75 million after expenses of $2.25 million were paid. That revenue would easily exceed the amount brought in by Struggling State's first gala and establish a blueprint that the university could use for other fundraising projects. "Nearly eight million dollars for one night's work," the VP told the president's cabinet. "You've got to admit that's a pretty good return on investment."

When the quotas were announced to DOs and university administrators, there was an immediate backlash. The numbers had been set without any input from those who actually worked in each area. Some DOs worked with a relatively large number of donors who gave very small amounts each year to the university. They were afraid that supporters who regularly gave only $10 or $100 to the university each year would not only balk at the $1,000 ticket price but also refrain from making their customary gift. "If the university can afford to throw a $1,000-a-plate party for itself," some donors would conclude, "it certainly doesn't need my pittance."

Other DOs worked with a donor base that could easily afford the tickets, but they all had relatively few donors assigned to them. "People who give $500,000 or a million dollars to the university each year require prolonged cultivation and stewardship," one DO said. "I don't even *have* five hundred names in my active client list."

Department chairs and deans were equally angered by the VP's plan. "I have an academic unit to run," many of them said. "I don't have time to go door to door selling tickets as though they were Girl Scout Cookies."

In addition, the provost pointed out to the VP for development that department chairs and deans frequently shared the exact same donor pools. "Where are a dean's hundred tickets going to come from?" one of the deans asked at a meeting with the provost. "They'll come from the same people to whom each chair is trying to sell his or her ten tickets. Or maybe they'd come from the advisory board if the advisory board didn't have to sell its own allotment of tickets. There's *no way* the university has 10,000 supporters who are each capable of spending $1,000 for a one-night event. This is Struggling State, after all."

The result was that morale sank in the division of development while tempers flared in the division of academic affairs. The VP made it clear that any DO who didn't meet the quota would not be retained for the following year. But when deans and department chairs learned that no sanction would be forthcoming if they failed to meet their quota—since the VP for development wasn't their supervisor, had few ways to reward them, and lacked any way to punish them—they simply ignored the target numbers entirely. Some administrators halfheartedly told faculty members and community supporters that tickets were available if they wanted them; others said nothing at all.

Two weeks before the gala the VP calculated that fewer than two thousand tickets had been sold. She called the DOs on the carpet and berated them for undermining her efforts and not sufficiently caring about their university. That was the final straw for several of the DOs who resigned on the spot.

Adopting a different tactic, the VP reduced the ticket price to $100 for members of the faculty and staff—angering the handful who had purchased their tickets at full price—and pleaded with the administrators to buy a block of these tickets with their development funds and give them out at no cost to anyone who would come.

The revised tactic began to make a difference and, by the night of the gala, 5,648 tickets had been sold, less than hoped for but still significantly more than the last two years. 1,945 of these tickets were sold at the full price of $1,000, with an additional 3,603 tickets sold at the reduced price of $100. The gross income from ticket sales was thus $2,305,300.

"I'd still call that a success," the VP for development said when reporting on the gala at the next meeting of the president's cabinet. "Sure we didn't meet our goal—*this* year. But we developed a plan that we can use to build from next year and the year after that. Besides, we took an event that had lost money for the last two years and made it profitable. I think that's something we can all take great pride in."

"Can we?" the provost asked. Eyes turned as this new jarring note was introduced at the conclusion of the upbeat speech from the VP for development. "Here's what I see as the result. You may indeed have sold well over three thousand reduced-price tickets, but the figures I'm seeing here show that 2,561 of the reduced-priced tickets were purchased through internal transfers of development funding.

In other words, the gala only brought in $2,049,200 in new money. When you subtract the $2.25 million in costs from that, it means that you actually lost nearly two hundred thousand dollars. That's two hundred thousand dollars less that my colleges and departments now have available to them in scholarship funding."

The provost then went on to enumerate other losses created by the event:

- Nearly three solid months of staff time in the division of development during which other fundraising activities were ignored.
- The resignation of several highly valued DOs who had together raised over thirty million dollars for the university during their careers.
- The alienation of a number of small donors who decided not to give the university anything this year because they couldn't afford the gala's high ticket price.
- Further loss caused by the need to clean and restore the basketball arena which had never been intended to accommodate over five thousand people on the court at once.

After the president reviewed the scenarios described by the two VPs, the VP for development was, in the institution's common euphemism, given her freedom to pursue other career opportunities.

Question: Is there anything an A Team could have done to achieve a more successful outcome?

Case Study Discussion

Because A Teams include representation from many segments of the university, they're highly unlikely to develop quotas in the way that the VP for development did in this case study. The academic officer (AO) would have pointed out that not all colleges and departments are the same size; thus setting numerically equal quotas for all units creates a plan that's likely to fail. Moreover, the AO and DO would have known each unit and its advisory board well enough to know the capacity of each to provide donors capable of purchasing a $1,000 ticket for a single event. They would have recognized how much the donor base of colleges overlapped with those of their departments and wouldn't have set unrealistic goals.

Because members of an A Team would have mastered the technique of building reasonable gift pyramids as we explored in Chapter 1, they wouldn't have pursued a strategy that required too many contributions of the same size for success. They might have sought, for instance, to secure sponsorships to cover the costs of food and entertainment so that the revenue from ticket sales was pure profit. They could have lowered the price of each ticket from $1,000 to, say, $400 and thus increased the likelihood of attracting 10,000 paying guests with a revenue to the university of four million dollars.

Moreover, they could have considered outsourcing the planning of the event to a professional event planning firm, thus leaving the development staff free to engage in other fundraising activities even while the gala was being planned. Finally, if a representative from athletics had been on the A Team, he or she would have pointed out the inadvisability of hosting large public events on an easily damaged basketball court.

Most important of all, the A Team probably would have recommended that a different type of fundraising activity be considered. Except at the most well financed and prestigious universities that happen to be located in areas where gala fatigue doesn't exist, the best strategy to follow after a successful gala is to *let that idea lie fallow for a few years and try to think of other inventive ways to raise money.*

F Troops are attracted to galas because they believe these events will result in quick income and abundant networking opportunities for administrators. The truth is, however, that galas not only have the disappointing return on investment that we saw earlier but also make it very difficult for any administrator to engage in meaningful discussions with people when loud music, other entertainment, speeches, and background conversation are all occurring simultaneously.

TOO MANY EGGS IN ONE BASKET

Fixation on galas is just one example of the tendency some institutions have to rely too much on a single development strategy. The common investment advice that you should "diversify your portfolio" is good guidance for an A Team as well. If you focus too exclusively on single events, ways of packaging a gift (such as remainder annuity trusts), or fundraising approaches (such as capital campaigns), your overall success is less likely to reach its full potential.

For example, building the endowment is a great long-term strategy, but if you don't have any expendable funds to use until this endowment matures, your program could lie fallow for several years. That's why A Teams tend to use what we call the *Denny's Grand Slam* approach, based on one of the most familiar items found at the famous chain of family restaurants. Some readers may recall the commercials produced by Denny's in the 1980s that described the restaurant's Grand Slam Breakfast: "Two large fresh eggs, two juicy sausage links, two strips of sizzling bacon, and two pancakes with hot syrup and butter" (see, for example, www.youtube.com/watch?v=rHzm40POUo0).

Good development portfolios use a very similar approach: not just endowment accounts, annual giving, deferred gifts, gifts-in-kind, or lead trusts, but a mixture of all the above. In other words, rather than putting all your eggs in one basket, sound strategy suggests that you have them share a plate with sausage, bacon, and pancakes, perhaps accompanied by some coffee and orange juice as well.

The very existence of an A Team is often enough to lead institutions away from too narrow a menu of strategies to achieve their fundraising goals. A dean is likely to have ideas that the VP for development doesn't. The marketing director, faculty representative to the research committee, and registrar will all see an issue from different perspectives. "Why are you thinking of unveiling this campaign at a separate event?" the athletic director may ask. "Why don't we do it during halftime at homecoming when we'll already have a live audience of about twenty thousand and many times that watching it on TV?"

Those varied perspectives can keep a team from going to the same well too many times, regardless of whether that "well" is the same small group of donors or the same tired fundraising strategy. The problem many institutions face is that certain strategies, like galas, work once or twice because they're seen by donors as new and exciting.

But by the time those same strategies have been used three or four years in a row, what was once regarded as innovative now seems mundane. The Denny's Grand Slam Approach gives an A Team enough variety in its strategies that donors are continually cultivated in new ways. Let's see how this approach could work in helping an institution that fell into the habit of storing all its (golden) eggs in one basket.

CASE STUDY #2

For many years, the development office at One Trick Pony College had been bringing in a small, relatively consistent revenue stream but not performing at a level that could truly transform the school. At last, the VP for development thought he had the answer. "We're spreading our efforts too thin. We're a small staff that can only cover a limited number of events. If you look at our schedule—with alumni weekend, family weekend, the local campaign, state campaign, national campaign, and all the rest—we're just trying to do too much and thus not doing any of them properly. We need to cut back from doing fifteen or twenty big projects each year to just one: a single, high profile event centered on an internationally known celebrity.

We'll book a politician or actor or major author, build the event around the celeb-rity, and gain a huge amount of publicity in the process. We'll sell tickets to the public event, higher priced tickets to a meet-and-greet with the celebrity, even higher priced tickets to a meal with the celebrity, and so on.

We'll focus all our fundraising efforts this year on this event. That way, we can con-solidate staff costs by hiring temporary workers for a phone bank a few weeks before and after the event, do the majority of our alumni calls then, and encourage people to increase their level of support in recognition of the increased prestige One Trick Pony College is going to have because of this new event. Sure, a person of the stature I'm talking about will charge $100,000 or more in fees, but that's nothing in comparison to the increased revenue this approach will yield."

The VP's idea received almost immediate approval from the president and develop-ment staff. A number of surveys and focus groups were held to determine what type of figure would have the name recognition and draw needed for the event to be suc-cessful. Eventually there was one name everyone could agree on: Sarah Bellum, most widely known for her role in the long-running Trek Wars franchise of movies. Older alumni remembered her fondly from early films in that series. Current students knew her as the kindly Auntie Bellum, as famous for her international work on behalf of human rights and her exercise videos as for her ongoing role in Trek Wars.

Over and over again, people responded, "Now, *her* I would pay to see" whenever her name came up. And so, even though the VP for development blanched a bit when Sarah Bellum's agent told him that the fee would be $250,000 for her to participate in all the events the college had planned for her, he agreed to that price. The college had done its homework and, if the gift pyramid they constructed had been at all realistic, the events would yield several million dollars in profit even after paying the actress' exorbitant fee.

Throughout the rest of that academic year and over the summer, the development staff met at least weekly to make certain that every detail was perfect. The events would all take place on October 10th. In order to build anticipation, cryptic emails began to be distributed in May with messages like "Are you ready for 10/10?" bla-zoned over the Trek Wars logo.

The college was determined to get the maximum impact for the high fee being charged by the actress. The institution's website and every one of its publication bore her image. First time contributors were promised a number of special privileges, such as the opportunity to purchase premium sports tickets and free admission to a cultural event of their choice, for a contribution of only $10.10. While no one pledged the ultimate gift—"Pony up by pledging ten million dollars to One Trick Pony College, payable over ten years, and have the Administration Building renamed Sarah Bellum Hall!"—the cleverness of that pitch brought in several new pledges and garnered a lot of free publicity.

It took until July for the first wrinkle in the VP of development's plan to appear. Several of the college's alumni who had long been large donors refused to make their customary gift. When asked about their change of heart, they would say things like, "I just don't agree with Sarah Bellum's politics" and "Don't you remember her 'peace mission' to the Taliban? I'm not going to have my name associated with someone like Sarah Bellum."

These statements worried the development VP because they meant that the highly publicized event might now only compensate for the loss of the alumni gifts he had counted on when planning his annual budget. But he figured that the college was still getting so much publicity that there was a chance the event could exceed its projected revenue. Besides, he had learned a valuable lesson: Despite the popularity of a figure like Sarah Bellum, next year he needed to give extra careful consideration to the names of the celebrities that people proposed in order to avoid this kind of unexpected opposition.

From that point onward, planning for the event proceed rather smoothly until just before noon on October 6th. The VP for development received a call that suddenly made his blood run cold: While filming her latest exercise video, Sarah Bellum had slipped and injured her back. She was currently in the hospital, unable to move. It would be impossible for her to participate in the October 10th event. Panicked, the VP for development tried every possibility he could think of. Could she participate via video? Could she at least phone in? Would the agent be willing to see if one of her costars from the Trek Wars series could fill in for her? No, no, and no. Exasperated by the agent's unwillingness to see this turn of events as a disaster for the college, the VP said that he expected a prompt refund of the $250,000 speaking fee, which had already been paid.

And it was then that what was already a disaster assumed truly apocalyptic proportions: The agent calmly referred to the clause in the contract the college had signed, making one major concession in return for the right to use the actress' image so broadly that year: In the event that Sarah Bellum was unable to participate in the event "through reasons beyond her control," she would still be entitled to full payment of the fee.

At the time the contract was negotiated, the VP assumed that this language had been added to the contract to protect the actress in case *the college* canceled the event (which it had no intention of doing). But he now saw the full impact of what he had signed. He had caused the college to pay a quarter of a million dollars for little more than the use of Sarah Bellum's image on its website and flyers. And that image had caused several large donors to withhold their gifts to the college.

Over the next twenty-four hours as word of Sarah Bellum's injury got out, the cancellations to the October 10th event rolled in. Pledges that had been made were rescinded. Nearly half of the gifts that had been paid were requested by donors to be returned. Local media had a field day with the college's embarrassment. A member of the town council was quoted in the newspaper as saying, "It looks as though One Trick Pony College put all of its eggs in one basket only to discover that the eggs were rotten and the basket never really existed."

The president worked valiantly with the VP for development to save the situation somehow. The president, although a highly introverted person who disliked large public events, agreed to appear in the actress' place and to make personal phone calls to each of the donors affected by the unexpected turn of events. Several of the alumni donors who had withheld their gifts out of protest against the college's involvement with Sarah Bellum came through with their contributions after all. It looked as though the college would end up having lost money, harmed its reputation, and expended its entire development budget for the year by the end of the first quarter, but not irreparably damaged. It had at least learned a valuable lesson.

But then came the coup de grace: Attorneys for the studio that produced the Trek Wars series informed One Trick Pony College that it was being sued for unauthorized use of the franchise's logo. The same contract that had bound the school to pay Sarah Bellum even though she never participated in the event had only purchased the rights to *her* image, not the logo of the Trek Wars series. On the advice of its attorneys, the college decided to avoid an expensive trial and settled with the studio out of court for an undisclosed sum. And the VP for development was immediately released from his contract.

Question: What advice do you give to the next VP for development?

Case Study Discussion

Recognizing that the college can't afford a second disaster, you recommend a strategy based on the Denny's Grand Slam approach. The college should return to a multi-pronged development strategy with perhaps not as many different events as it had attempted previously but certainly more than a single "all in" campaign. An A Team is put together including the new VP for development, the president, several deans, the alumni director, and the director of marketing. The group brainstorms various possible approaches and finally decides to build in a "failsafe" mechanism to each event it plans for the near future, knowing that the local media would pounce on any failure that reminds them in any way of the Sarah Bellum event. The ideas proceed along several lines.

For example, one month the development office will choose a random name from its list of donors and offer that person two free spots on that year's affinity tour. (On affinity travel programs, see Chapter 5 of the companion volume to this book, *Going for the Gold: How to Become a World-Class Academic Fundraiser*, 2016.)

At several other times throughout the year, the president or chair of the board of trustees will make phone calls to personally thank donors who have contributed at various levels. Periodically, other donors will receive elaborately decorated cakes on their birthday. After each one of these events, the college will take full advantage of the publicity it generates by describing the result through social media and television stations in several key markets.

The failsafe mechanism put in place is that the college will only pursue this publicity *if the event is successful*. If the results are disappointing—if, for example, the recipient of the birthday cake is displeased because he or she has just gone on a diet—the college will simply ignore the event and no one will be the wiser. By taking this course of action, the college is so successful that, within a decade, it changes its name to Multifaceted University and offers you a position on its executive leadership team.

The lesson to be drawn from the two case studies we've examined so far in this chapter is that fundraising strategies need to be sound in their conception and execution, varied from time to time because even the most wonderful event can begin to feel like "just another obligation" if it's repeated too often, and not depended on for too much of the budget because things don't always work out as planned.

A central strategy of an A Team is that it not only is creative in developing innovate strategies but also flexible in developing *lots* of strategies. In the language of Archilochus' famous dictum about the fox and the hedgehog—"The fox knows many tricks, the hedgehog just one important trick."—an A Team is definitely the fox. Hedgehogs find it hard to survive in the unpredictable and ever-changing world of academic fundraising.

STRATEGIES THAT FIT—AND THOSE THAT DON'T

The fundraising strategies that an institution pursues have to make sense in terms of its mission and identity. A religious institution might conclude that a summer festival featuring alcoholic beverages, gambling, and students in revealing bathing suits is just not suitable for the values it represents. A college with a strong commitment to human rights might be humiliated if it was discovered that the gifts it offered its large donors were the products of child labor in a developing country.

Not all mismatches of strategy and mission are this obvious, but an A Team is always asking questions like, "Is this project appropriate in terms of who we are?" not, as an F Troop might ask, merely "Can we make a lot of money doing this?" Even when not dealing with a project's overall strategy, members of an A Team are sensitive to the interests and mindsets of their audience.

While members of an F Troop might fill their presentations with sports metaphors and allusions to last night's game, members of an A Team don't automatically assume that everyone they're talking to is fond of sports. While members of an F Troop might assume that every prospective donor has gone to college and understands the structure and terminology of higher education, members of an A Team subtly embed explanations in what they say and write.

Saying something like, "Our provost, who heads all the academic programs at the university ..." gently informs listeners who don't know what a provost does, but doesn't insult the intelligence of those who do.

Making sure that the strategies used in fundraising suit both the interests of the donor and the character of the institution is not only a matter of being respectful to those who support your programs; it's also an effective practice.

BOX 3.2

Fundraising is a lot like matchmaking. You're not really successful unless each party thinks that he or she got the better deal.

If a donor comes away from a meeting feeling as though the university representative acted like a disreputable car salesman, it's not going to be a satisfactory experience for everyone even if the gift is ultimately made. It's far better for the team to approach their work as a public service in which they help those with philanthropic intent find the *right* cause to support, not merely *any* cause. In so doing, the group is much more likely to pursue a strategy that strengthens the relationship between the donor and the institution.

CASE STUDY #3

You're meeting with your team to discuss which fundraising strategy to pursue for which program during this year's development campaign. Since you don't want to repeat strategies so often that they lose their effectiveness, you choose only one strategy to use per program. While there are several different ways of matching strategies and programs that produce "right" answers, there are also a number of combinations that are clearly inadvisable.

We'll admit that this particular team has a pretty unusual combination of programs for which it's responsible. But your goal is to find what you believe is the best strategy for each of the ten programs listed below. Read over all the programs and strategies and then put the letter of the strategy that you'd use to raise funds for that particular program. Remember: You want to use each strategy only once.

Programs

1. *The College of Business Administration*. A large college that includes programs in management, marketing, accounting, hospitality management, sports management, and general business.
2. *The College of Education*. A mid-sized college that produces elementary and secondary school teachers and enrolls a sizable number of first-generation college students.
3. *The School for the Performing Arts*. A sub-unit of the College of Liberal Arts that includes the departments of theater, music, and dance.
4. *The Department of Interior Design*. One of the institution's smallest programs, preparing students to become design professionals in a highly competitive marketplace.
5. *The Department of Construction Management*. A program that teaches its students how to supervise building design projects, manage resources, interpret contracts and local safety standards, and bring ambitious construction plans to fruition.
6. *The Department of History*. A department that serves only a few majors and graduate students each year but has a high service load because of its contribution to the general education program.
7. *The Peace and Justice Institute*. An interdisciplinary academic program that studies the issues of peace, conflict, and justice throughout the world and seeks to develop recommendations for promoting a more equitable world.
8. *The Creativity Institute*. An interdisciplinary academic program that seeks to develop innovative solutions to complex problems and analyze the processes that lead to innovative discoveries.
9. *Leadership Education & Academic Development (LEAD)*. A service program through which the institution helps improve the leadership and problem-solving skills of faculty members and administrators.
10. *University High School*. A fully accredited high school for high ability students who dual enroll in certain college classes while completing the requirements for their secondary school diplomas.

Strategies

a. *Change for the Better*. Students from the program will staff the exits to the football stadium, basketball court, and hockey arena. When fans leave the event, they'll be encouraged to contribute all their loose change to the project.
b. *The Write Stuff*. A major author will be brought to campus to talk about and give readings from his or her current work in progress. Admission to the event will be high, with an even higher price charged to those who want to meet privately with the author at a cocktail reception following the presentation.

c. *Personal Assistant for a Day.* Volunteers from the football, hockey, field hockey, softball, and cheerleading teams will auction their labor to the highest bidder. The winning bidder will be able to use the student-athlete, accompanied by a school representative, for one day in performing a set menu of activities, including house-cleaning, meal preparation, dog-walking, and the like.

d. *Dean for a Day.* The winning bidder will "fill in" for one of the college deans for a day, with an agenda of pleasant (and completely unofficial) activities planned.

e. *The Educated Palate.* The winning bidder will have the services of the entire dining hall staff who will prepare a lavish banquet for up to fifty guests at the alumni center.

f. *After a Fashion.* An elegant fashion show, presenting the latest styles from some of the world's foremost designers. The event will have a high ticket price, with a special reception for those who purchase premium tickets.

g. *Mind and Body.* A luxury river cruise through the French wine country with daily cultural presentations by faculty members, a complete massage package, and gourmet meals.

h. *Presidential Perks.* An opportunity to spend a full day with the school's president, including skybox seats at a home football game, front row seats at an evening lecture by a Nobel laureate, and dinner at the faculty club.

i. *One-on-One.* Donors to this program pay the equivalent of one student's tuition, room, and board for a year. In return, they receive regular email updates from the student, monthly invitations to join the student at lunch or dinner, and a personal invitation to join the student at a special event when he or she graduates.

j. *Buying Time.* This program enables donors to buy the naming rights to certain campus facilities—such as the stadium, the field within the stadium, the basketball arena, the court within the arena, certain classroom buildings and residence halls, fountains, and the like—for set periods of one, five, ten, twenty, or twenty-five years. After the period elapses, the institution would be permitted to sell those naming rights to a different donor.

Case Study Discussion

As was said previously, there's no single right way to assign the strategies to these pro-grams. But if we pay attention to how different strategies fit different programs, there are a number of wrong assignments we could make:

- The College of Business Administration is probably best paired with a strategy that suits its mission of preparing the business leaders of tomorrow. Dean for a Day, Presidential Perks, and Buying Time all make sense from this perspective. Change for the Better, Mind and Body, and One-on-One are probably less suitable choices.
- Since the College of Education enrolls many first-generation college students, One-on-One would be an excellent strategy for this program. Change for the Better and Buying Time might also be appropriate choices. The Educated Palate, After a Fashion, and Mind and Body don't seem to lend themselves very well to this school's mission.
- The Write Stuff seems a natural choice for the School for the Performing Arts. After a Fashion, Personal Assistant for a Day, and Buying Time might also be appropriate. Less satisfactory choices include Dean for a Day and Presidential Perks.
- The best choice for the Department of Interior Design is probably After a Fashion. Personal Assistant for a Day, the Educated Palate, and Mind and Body would also

be appropriate strategies. Change for the Better and One-on-One don't appear to have an obvious connection to this program.

- The Department of Construction Management would probably be well served by Dean for a Day, Presidential Perks or Buying Time. Less satisfactory strategies would be Change for the Better, After a Fashion, and Mind and Body.
- The Department of History would be well served by Change for the Better, the Write Stuff, or Mind and Body. Strategies that don't have an obvious fit for this department's mission include Personal Assistant for a Day and After a Fashion.
- The best strategy for the Peace and Justice Institute is probably Change for the Better. One-on-One and Buying Time could work as well. Personal Assistant for a Day doesn't just seem unsuited to this program's mission; its very focus—"exploiting" the labor of others for money—might be regarded as completely antithetical to that mission. Similarly the Educated Palate and Mind and Body don't seem suitable to this program's emphasis on justice and equity for all.
- The Creativity Institute has a mission that fits well with the Write Stuff, After a Fashion, and Mind and Body. In fact, none of the strategies seems wholly unsuited to this program, although it may be a stretch to find a logical connection to Personal Assistant for a Day and Presidential Perks.
- LEAD would best be served by strategies that have some connection with leadership, such as Dean for a Day and Presidential Perks. The Educated Palate and After a Fashion are probably not the best strategies to pursue.
- Change for the Better and One-on-One would probably work well for University High School. Personal Assistant for a Day and After a Fashion don't appear to reflect the program's mission very well.

For a somewhat different approach to choosing strategies for specific fundraising goals—the use of data instead of a focus on mission and fit—see Birkholz (2008).

CONCLUDING THOUGHTS

The mistakes that F Troops make when it comes to strategy fall into three main categories:

1. They choose strategies that just don't work.
2. They choose strategies that work but then overuse them.
3. They choose strategies that work but that don't fit the mission of the institution or program for which they're working.

The broad range of expertise found in an A Team helps eliminate these mistakes. Those with deep knowledge of the academic program have a sense of which strategies just don't feel right in terms of the values and goals of the unit. Those with extensive training and experience in fundraising know which strategies tend to be effective and which require more effort than they're worth. Those with creativity and an entrepreneurial spirit bring a willingness to try new ideas and keep the group's fundraising plans fresh, eliminating the need to try the same tired strategies over and over again.

REFERENCES

Birkholz, J. (2008). *Fundraising analytics: Using data to guide strategy*. Hoboken, NJ: Wiley

Buller, J. L., & Reeves, D. M. (2016). *Going for the gold: How to become a world-class academic fundraiser*. Lanham, MD: Rowman & Littlefield.

Greenfield, J. M. (1999). *Fund raising: Evaluating and managing the fund development process*. New York, NY: Wiley.

RESOURCES

Buller, J. L. (2007). "But I hate asking for money...": Development Tips for Academic Administrators. *Academic Leader. 23*(8), 1, 6.

Grace, K. S. (2009). *Fundraising mistakes that bedevil all boards (and staff too): A 1-hour guide to identifying and overcoming obstacles to your success*. (Rev. ed.) Medfield, MA: Emerson & Church.

Klingaman, S. (2012). *Fundraising strategies for community colleges: The definitive guide for advancement*. Sterling, VA: Stylus.

Chapter Four

The Challenge of Loose Cannons

As we'll see repeatedly throughout this chapter and the next, volunteers can play a vital role in academic fundraising. They bring a perspective that the people who work at or attend a college or university may lack. They can be viewed by prospective donors as far more objective about an institution than the faculty, staff, and administration can be. And they can help fill staffing gaps, at least on a limited basis, when there aren't enough employees available to address every need.

But volunteers can also create enormous challenges, and the skill used in addressing those challenges is one of the factors that separate the A Teams from the F Troops. For example, advisory boards tend to start out being very effective but then lapse into offering advice about matters beyond their scope of responsibility. They may even try to start acting like governing boards and "decide" matters that, at most, they should be making recommendations on.

Governing boards, too, can begin to drift beyond their original charge, interfering in the day-to-day operations of the institution, and trying to help with fundraising in ways that aren't really helpful. A Teams are adept at shifting the focus of these volunteers back to their true responsibilities without making them feel foolish or unappreciated. F Troops either act too aggressively and thus alienate the volunteers or not assertively enough and thus allow the volunteers to function as loose cannons.

Loose cannons aren't limited to volunteers, of course. There are faculty members who go off on their own and proudly secure a $500,000 gift that gets in the way of the *$50 million gift* the school was trying to secure from the same donor. Academic administrators can be loose cannons, giving interviews to local media that, because of an ill-chosen remark, cause donors to rescind their pledges.

Development officers (DOs) can be loose cannons when they filch one another's prospects either because they don't follow procedures or think they could get away with this violation of professional ethics. In this chapter, we'll explore several of these loose cannon scenarios, beginning with the one that launched this discussion: the volunteer who oversteps established boundaries.

CASE STUDY #1

One college of a large university was housed entirely on a regional campus about eighty miles away from the institution's primary location. While this separation caused some challenges, it wasn't a deterrent to the faculty, staff, and students in that particular program. The college had just celebrated its twentieth anniversary and was highly regarded in the region for its innovative, highly entrepreneurial academic offerings. Credit for this success was partly due to the school's advisory board whose main function had been to help raise public awareness of the college and increase financial support for its facilities, scholarships, professorships, and program support.

After the founding dean, a highly respected scholar in her field, retired after thirteen years of service, the college was led by an interim dean for two years. This interim period had not been intended to last that long, but the search for a new dean with a record as distinguished as the college's founder had proven to be difficult.

Throughout this transition, the advisory board helped fill the resulting leadership void. It stepped up its fundraising efforts, served as the college's public image to external stakeholders, and (in a way that was unusual at the institution) even played a key role in screening and interviewing candidates for the deanship. The chair of the advisory board, a retired executive who was a thoughtful person with a commanding presence, provided a great deal of strategic guidance that helped the college keep moving forward.

One clique on the board became particularly influential. All were retired chief executive officers or senior administrators. Once a permanent dean had been hired, members of this group seemed reluctant to surrender the type of hands-on leadership they had demonstrated while the search was under way. They advocated forcefully for building additional space that could be used for faculty and administrative offices (including a lavish new dean's suite) and house a 250-seat experimental theater that could help kick start a performing arts program in the college.

The group seemed preoccupied with the idea of using this new facility to launch a music series for the community even though two other venues in the area were already providing a full calendar of professional performances in theater, music, and dance. While the new dean and the college's faculty responded politely to the board's concept for a new facility, it didn't rank very high on their list of priorities and so three years went by without the concept even being mentioned in the unit's annual budget request.

On its own, therefore, the sub-group of the college's advisory board drafted a case statement that included some highly questionable statistics to justify the need for the building. Coincidentally, the governing board of the university happened to be engaged in one of its periodic updates to the institution's master plan for facilities. In a meeting about the future of the regional campus where the college was located, the dean and his DO described the need for expanded space for certain academic programs, but once again made no mention of the new office facility with its experimental theater.

One member of the college's advisory board who saw himself as the champion of the new facility had a close business relationship with several members of the governing board. When he learned that the project had yet again been ignored by the college's administration, he met privately with the people he knew on the governing board, argued strongly in its favor, and requested that, if institutional funding wasn't allocated for the project, he be given permission to start a fundraising campaign that would defray the cost of construction and demonstrate the community's support for the idea.

Thinking they had been given a convenient way out of an awkward situation, the members of the governing board told him that that was a great plan: He should first raise at least half the cost of the project privately and only then come back to them about including the concept on the master plan.

The advisory board member thus began to consider himself on a mission. He approached various members of the college staff and demanded information from them about current plans for programming, the cost per square foot of existing facilities, the school's donor list, and enrollment projections. When he didn't get answers immediately, he became abusive with the staff and demanded to speak to their supervisors. He claimed that he had influence with the dean and would make sure that their "rude treatment of an important community member" was reflected in their evaluations. He even implied that he might cost a few employees their jobs.

When the dean learned what was going on, he assured the staff that he valued their work, didn't intend to give them poor evaluations, and was sorry they'd had such an unpleasant experience. He said that their first priorities had to be meeting the needs of the students and faculty of the college and, only if they had free time available, should they concern themselves with the board member's requests. Besides, he reminded them, some of the information the board member wanted was confidential and *couldn't* be released.

This approach calmed the staff, and a plan was developed that, whenever the board member approached them for additional information, they would respond that he needed to speak with the dean who was responsible for approving their work assignments.

At the next meeting of the college's advisory board, the DO gave, as though it were part of her ongoing training of the board, an overview of how work was assigned to the college's staff. She noted that people were hired for specific duties and that anything that went above and beyond those duties needed to be approved in advance by the dean and those requests that consumed their time for special projects must be approved in advance by the dean.

The board member seemed irritated by the tactic used by the dean and DO, but said nothing about it at the time. Nevertheless, a month later, he sent a registered letter to the university's president, essentially demanding that the school move ahead with the project. In his letter, the board member misrepresented the amount of support the idea had from the college's advisory board, claimed that there was a window of opportunity that would be lost if the project didn't begin quickly, and attached the case statement for the project that hadn't been approved by the dean or development staff.

When the president's office contacted the college to find out more about the situation, the dean decided that trying to humor the board member had only made the matter worse. He called a meeting with the board member, the advisory board chair, the college's DO, and himself. When the group gathered, the board chair, who had previously been so effective in that role, said almost nothing and let the dean run the meeting.

Trying to control his frustration, the dean pointed out that several board members had contacted him out of concern that their names had been included in the letter that was sent to the president, even though they didn't want to pursue the project if it wasn't a priority for the college. As diplomatically as possible, the dean noted that the board member had done valuable work for the college in the past when he simplified the school's financial reporting and developed specific metrics to measure the board's effectiveness.

But he noted that there were limits to the roles and responsibilities of the advisory board and that the member's recent actions had blatantly ignored those limits. He asked the board member whether he had any continuing interest in being a board member now that the group's function had been clarified to him. Ignoring the question, the board member noted that, as a citizen and donor, he had every right to contact other members of the administration and state his views, particularly when he believed the college's administration was making a serious mistake.

"That may be true" the dean replied, "but you *don't* have the right to say that you're speaking on behalf of the board when you actually aren't." The tone of the meeting became increasingly tense until finally the board member declared that perhaps it wasn't a good fit for him to remain on the advisory board "under the current administration." "I accept your resignation," the dean replied, gathering up his papers and then leaving the room.

The following day, four other members of the board resigned, stating that they couldn't continue working for the college in an advisory capacity if their advice was going to be ignored. The advisory board, which had once been such a crucial part of the college's activity, seemed to lose all momentum following this event. It continued to meet for two more years but never regained its former energy.

Eventually, the dean dissolved the college's advisory board, leaving some of its members feeling that they had wasted their time working with the group ever since the new dean was hired. Several formerly significant contributors stopped making gifts to the university.

Question: Could an A Team have done anything different to achieve a better outcome?

Case Study Discussion

What this case study illustrates for us is that, when it comes to loose cannons, you can't wait too long to intervene. The longer a loose cannon remains unchecked, the more damage it does and the "looser" it tends to become: Failing to put a stop to destructive activities is regarded as tacit approval, and the person's behavior becomes even worse. If an A Team had been involved in this situation, it probably would never have reached the level of severity it did. Early in his position, the dean would have thanked the advisory board sincerely for the leadership role it played during the college's transition.

The dean would note that, now that a new administrator was in charge, he would be setting the college's priorities for the future, and the board could return to its original advisory role, particularly in such areas as raising the visibility of the college and securing external funds; facilities, curricular matters, personnel issues, and the like would all be addressed internally by the administration.

If that didn't prove to be a sufficient approach and the board member kept interfering in administrative policy matters, the dean would have thanked the member sincerely for his services and then released him from further service on the advisory board.

Doing so at an early point in the process may cause some hard feelings in the short term, but it helps avoid the long-term damage that such a person is capable of causing. In addition, it sends a message to the board that the dean truly is in charge of major decisions concerning the college's future and appointments to the advisory board. Several other members, who had risen to fill what they perceived as a leadership void, may even have been relieved to discover that they could return to an advisory role.

At the point where the story ended, however, serious damage had already been done. At this point, the best thing that one can do is to let a few years go by and then reconstitute a new advisory board that adheres more fully to the principles that we'll outline in the next chapter.

Term limits, for example, are a particularly effective way of preventing loose cannons from getting too far out of control. In addition, clear bylaws, mission statements, and operating procedures make it clear that certain matters are within the board's purview, while certain matters aren't. Then, when a member begins to express views about matters that go beyond these stated limits, the appropriate member of the A Team can gently remind the person about the guidelines contained in the operating procedures he or she agreed to when first joining the board.

CONFLICTS IN VALUES

Like any institution, a college or university will contain people who have very different ideals, perspectives, and values. Higher education, however, places a great deal of emphasis on ideological diversity and often takes specific steps during the recruitment of faculty and students to make sure that an appropriately rich mix of people becomes part of the community. Exposure to a wide range of ideas is part of higher education's mission, after all: It seeks to expose people to those with backgrounds different from their own, individuals who believe different things from what they believe and who approach the core questions of life in fundamentally different ways.

While seminaries and faith-based institutions do exist within the system of higher education and dedicate themselves to propagating, not challenging certain belief systems, even they are part of the broad diversity that can be found in higher education today because they offer their stakeholders a choice. If students, faculty members, and donors want to become involved in a very small, private, undergraduate college in a rural community that only enrolls students of a specific gender, they can find a school that fills that need. If they want to attend a huge, public, urban university where most people maintain an exclusively secular perspective and are progressive on social issues, they can find that, too, as well as nearly every possible combination and permutation one might think of.

The people with whom we interact in higher education don't become loose cannons simply because they have values different from ours. They may, however, create problems when they assume that everyone else must share their beliefs and adopt only their perspectives on major issues.

Conflicts in values can arise in fundraising when a prospective donor insists that a project must be undertaken in a way that runs counter to the goals inherent in an institution's mission. And they can also arise when members of the faculty, staff, or administration allow someone's difference of perspective in one area blind them to a possibility of doing something positive in some other area where such conflicts don't exist.

A Teams understand that it's extraordinarily rare for any group of people to share beliefs and convictions on every single topic. In most of the things we do every day, this lack of agreement doesn't matter. Most people wouldn't refuse to dine in a particular restaurant or take their laundry to a particular cleaner because they a suspect that the owner of the restaurant votes differently from the way they do or the dry cleaner is a member of a different religion.

But sometimes people involved in academic life become "purists" when it comes to philanthropy: They feel uneasy accepting a gift from someone with a different outlook, even if that outlook has nothing at all to do with the gift. Certainly, the reputation and integrity of a potential donor has to be considered, and in specific cases these factors can become an obstacle because they could damage the school's reputation or bring it unfavorable publicity.

At other times, however, hoping that you can wait until you're offered exactly the right gift by someone who shares all of your convictions will get in the way of even the most basic of your fundraising goals. Most importantly, differences of *preference* that are mistaken for serious *moral* differences have to be set aside for the good of the institution as a whole. If they're not, they can derail an entire cultivation process.

In the next case study that we'll consider, the central question is what kind of difference exists in this situation? Is it serious enough to forego the gift, or is it one of those matters where the school and the donor can simply agree to disagree? In short, who is the loose cannon in this situation: the prospective donor or the school's president?

CASE STUDY #2

The president of a liberal arts college, accompanied by one of his deans, the chair of the performing arts department, and a DO, arrived for dinner with a wealthy couple in an exclusive gated community. The wife, Zoe, was an alumna of the college who's had a lifelong interest in performing arts. She remained involved with the college since her graduation twenty years earlier by attending several events each year and making small annual gifts. Her husband, Jack, was a businessman whose success allowed him to retire early. Since that time, he'd become highly active on a number of conservative political issues and had made a few unsuccessful runs for office at the state level. The couple had no children and, when Zoe came to campus for events, she always arrived alone.

The team was meeting with Zoe and Jack to see if they could secure preliminary support for a small "black-box" theater that would be useful as both a classroom and a venue for experimental performances. The evening began well with polite conversation about how well the college was doing recently, the profile of the incoming class, and a few of Zoe's other activities. Whenever it was appropriate, members of the team guided the conversation toward the growing theater program and the poor conditions of the performance space it was currently using.

As dinner progressed, it became clear that the couple was indeed interested in the idea of having its name associated with a new facility, and Zoe surprised the team by proposing that the concept be even larger: She said that she and Jack would also consider providing some scholarship support and an endowed position for a new professor of theater history, as long as terms could be worked out and the project timed to coordinate with their other philanthropic efforts. It was agreed that representatives of the college would meet again with the couple very soon and introduce them to some of the students and professors in the program.

It was over dessert that the mood in the room changed abruptly. Since it was a presidential election year, Jack began to talk about some of his work on behalf of candidates who, in his estimation, could provide strong congressional support to what he was convinced would be a socially and economically conservative president. The members of the team knew that the college's stakeholders represented a broad spectrum of political views and, even though Jack's philosophy didn't align with their own, remained non-committal as he talked about the need to rein in funding for social programs and "to do exactly what you all are doing here tonight: looking for private support for what you believe in, not relying on government handouts."

The team felt a little more uncomfortable as Jack expressed his opposition to higher education's "fixation on diversity" and "its obvious decision to hire only liberals and radicals for faculty positions." Jack then warmed to his subject and, perhaps influenced by the cognac he was consuming with his dessert, stated his opposition to what the president and his team considered central values of the college: equal opportunity, salary equity for men and women, reproductive choice, marriage equality, international cooperation, religious tolerance, and comprehensive health care.

The team tried to preserve as positive an atmosphere as possible. The dean spoke about the pedagogical value in having a diverse faculty and staff and said the idea that all college professors were liberals was "more a media illusion than fact." The president said that he personally welcomed a marketplace of ideas where all perspectives were welcome and noted that his own wife was currently serving as the executive director of a women's health center that included access to gender-specific health issues, pregnancy, abortion counseling, and helping transsexuals deal with issues of self-identity and social acceptance.

Jack's immediate response seemed softer than the tone of many of his remarks. "Well, we're all entitled to our own ideas." But then he continued, "Of course, she'll need to give up that kind of nonsense if we're going to fund this project. We'll want to be able to choose the professor who holds this chair so that we know he's the sort of person who's not taken in by all that liberal gobbledygook. In fact, I already have someone in mind. We need to get your students reading more Ayn Rand and Whittaker Chambers, not trash like Henry Miller, John Maynard Keynes, Tom Stoppard, and Eve Ensler."

The chair of the performing arts department bristled a bit because three of the four liberal authors whom Jack mentioned were playwrights whose works were regularly performed at the college. The president said cryptically, "Well, I think that tells us exactly what we needed to know."

The goodbyes were abrupt, and the college's president was fuming on the drive home. "If higher education is going to mean anything in this country, it's going to have to *stand* for something, not just kowtow to anyone with a checkbook. We're judged by the values of the people who support us, and I want nothing to do with anyone whose gift would come to us with strings attached, especially when those strings would prevent us from pursuing our most basic ideals."

The DO continued to urge follow-up conversations with Jack and Zoe, but the president expressly forbade the staff from continuing to work with the couple. Zoe and Jack took the president's action as a personal rejection of them and their beliefs. Zoe's attendance at campus events gradually dwindled as did the size of her annual contribution. Within a few years Jack and Zoe weren't involved with the college in any way.

Questions: What went wrong in this process? Whose fault was it? And could an A Team have had a better outcome?

Case Study Discussion

This case presents a more challenging situation than the first case study we considered in this chapter. It raises a fundamental question that frequently arises in academic fundraising: How much should an institution be willing to bend its principles in the interest of achieving a greater good?

In this particular situation, the donors were willing to make a substantial gift that could benefit numerous students, add a much-needed facility, and bring the college a fully funded faculty position. But one of the people providing that gift advocates ideas that run counter to the college's mission and has expectations for the gift that may require the college to sacrifice some of its more cherished principles.

This case is particularly interesting since, when we assign it in workshops, we find that academic officers (AOs) and DOs often end up on opposite sides of the issue. AOs tend to see this case as revolving around an issue of values; like the president in the story, they feel that accepting the gift or perhaps even continuing the conversation would constitute a betrayal of something vital to the school's mission and thus be completely inappropriate.

DOs tend to see this case as being one in which the academic side of the institution misunderstands how many people in the world act and state their positions. They argue that the president is really the loose cannon here: Rather than continuing the conversation and determining where some common ground may lie, he took Jack's bombast at face value and concluded that further discussions would be at best unproductive, at worst a public relations nightmare for the institution.

Certainly, no one would suggest that the college accept a gift that came with requirements that it turn its back on values central to its identity, dictates which causes members of the community will be allowed to support, or specifies who is to fill an endowed faculty position. But is that what's actually occurring in this case? What staff members in development know from experience but academic administrators may not realize is that donors *frequently* begin a project with certain stipulations in mind that fall by the wayside as discussions continue.

Naomi Levine, recently retired executive director of New York University's George H. Heyman, Jr. Center for Philanthropy and Fundraising, was quoted in a *Wall Street Journal* article that touched upon the subject of wealthy individuals, in this case, David and Charles Koch, whose gifts might trigger claims of political, ideological support or even tainted gifts. These claims might be generated by those who are in opposition to how the money was made that has traveled a pipeline to benefit an organization the donors support.

Levine noted that having processes approved by a Board of Directors in place will help the organization to determine whether to proceed with gifts that might bring controversy. "I don't know the politics of many of our donors," Levine said. "I suspect many of them have politics that I would be unhappy with. But that's irrelevant. If the money comes to us made legally and allows us to do with it what the university needs, we will accept it" (West, 2014).

In a subsequent email exchange with the authors, Levine clarified this observation. "However, if the donor has stated racist comments or is known as an anti-Semite, etc., that would clearly influence our decision to turn such a gift down. I believe it is important that every gift be judged individually. While a process helps making a decision, the facts are also critical" (Levine, 2016).

Each organization must make its own determination where to draw the line if a gift might bring forth moral or ethical contradictions. For instance, a LBGTQ (Lesbian, Bisexual, Gay, Transgender, Questioning) friendly organization is unlikely to accept a gift from a person who spews anti-gay rhetoric from any platform available.

Prospective donors may not understand many aspects of how higher education works. They may assume that, if they're the ones funding a new faculty line, they get to decide who is hired for that position, if they're paying for a new facility, they get to specify the architect, or if they endow a program, they're entitled to dictate how values are taught in that program.

A key part of the cultivation phase in academic fundraising is educating potential donors about what they can and can't control once a gift has been made. In this particular case, it's perfectly possible that many of Jack's demands were more rhetorical than serious in nature and could have been ironed out as discussions went forward. After all, it appears that alcoholic beverages had been plentiful, and, over dessert, Jack was simply launching into a speech he'd given many times. Even then, he himself may not have expected that the college representatives would take him seriously about every detail.

The real problem seems to have been the president's assumption that what we might call an initial negotiating position was identical to what the couple would have included in the final gift agreement. By breaking off the discussion, the president may well have deprived his college of an important gift that wouldn't, in the end, have caused the school to compromise any of its ideals.

If an A Team had been involved, someone with more experience with how these conversations evolve could perhaps have spoken to the president and persuaded him to continue the process at least until it could be determined how much flexibility Jack and Zoe would allow. After all, they had something significant to gain from this gift as well: Their name would be on the new facility. In such situations, donors are frequently willing to adjust what may initially have appeared to be non-negotiable demands.

Some readers may object, of course, because a figure as public as Jack could bring undesirable associations to the college if his remarks on television or in the newspaper were seriously at odds with the values embedded in the college's mission. To be sure, several institutions have had to deal with problems arising from facilities named after people who were later found to be racists, involved in illegal activities, or the advocates of highly objectionable moral principles.

If that concern arose among an A Team in the current scenario, the members would want to conduct due diligence on Jack's public remarks and consider how visible he is in the local or national media. If Jack were indeed likely to become widely known for points of view diametrically opposed to the college's core values, then it still may want to consider later during the negotiations whether it's wise to accept the couple's gift. However, if Jack were more likely to remain a strictly private citizen whose views didn't accord with those of the administration or many faculty members, then closing the door on further discussions seems rash.

No college or university is ever free of donors who believe things that at least some of their stakeholders may object to. It's the visibility of the platform from which those statements are delivered that is likely to be the real focus for an A Team.

GOOD INTENTIONS

So far in this chapter, we've seen the damage that loose cannons can do when they're volunteers, administrators, and (perhaps to a lesser extent) donors. But what can happen if the loose cannons you have to deal with are the DOs themselves? There are several ways in which members of the development staff can create problems by acting too independently. DOs can become loose cannons if they

- Get in over their heads by making commitments they're not authorized to make or decisions they don't fully understand.
- Try to play one potential donor against another in an effort to elicit a larger donation from one or both of them.
- Fail to coordinate with the rest of the development staff about their plans and intentions.
- Communicate poorly with other DOs and employees of the institution with the result that people are blindsided by matters that relate directly to their responsibilities.

Unfortunately, these scenarios are not particularly uncommon. But we can reduce their severity with a little bit of common sense. We have to remember that every member of an A Team is also a member of at least one other team. A dean is also a member of the college that he or she leads. A marketing director is also a member of the school's marketing or public relations team. And a DO is also a member of the institution's entire advancement team.

As such, the DO needs to make sure that he or she communicates effectively, not only with all the other members of the A Team, but with the rest of the development staff as well. In our next case study, we'll explore some of the results that can arise when a DO and other institutional employees fail to meet this very reasonable expectation.

CASE STUDY #3

The College of Musical Knowledge had a development office that was staffed with three DOs who worked closely with the school's faculty and the external board that oversaw the college's foundation. One of these DOs, Jim Bass, met a successful entrepreneur, Mr. Baton, at a meeting of one of the area's local service organizations. Mr. Baton had played several instruments when he was in college and earned a minor in music history.

As their conversations continued, it became clear that Mr. Baton could be persuaded to make an estate gift to the college of more than a million dollars, which could be used for faculty and student support in its music program, band uniforms, and travel funding so that the band and ensembles could perform at various venues. Since Mr. Baton also had interest in athletics, he might be further persuaded to make part of this gift early, so that he could enjoy the fruits of his generosity whenever the marching band played at sporting events.

Since the bulk of the contribution would come as a bequest, however, Bass turned the negotiations over to Sara Piccolo, another of the school's DOs who was a specialist in estate planning and deferred giving. Piccolo learned that Mr. Baton had also amassed a sizable collection of scores, books, and vintage instruments that his family had no interest in maintaining. As a result, she discussed with Mr. Baton the idea of expanding the gift even further: The gifts-in-kind would be donated now along with an expendable cash fund to maintain them and provide for new band uniforms; the bulk of the cash donation would be made through Mr. Baton's will.

Before a gift agreement could be finalized, however, Mr. Baton left the area for his summer home in Colorado. Part of the delay in drafting the agreement was the number of approvals it had to receive before it was submitted to the donor. The agreement was first reviewed by the college's legal counsel, next by the president's executive staff, and finally by the president herself. The president relied heavily on the advice of her chief-of-staff, an attorney who prided himself on making certain that the college exposed itself to as little risk as possible.

Weeks turned into months, and Piccolo became concerned that a valuable opportunity was being wasted. She called the president's secretary and chief-of-staff repeatedly, but never received a response other than "It's being reviewed." She tried to enlist Jim Bass' help because he had been Mr. Baton's first contact, but was told only, "This project is yours now. I wouldn't know where to begin."

Finally, Piccolo learned that the president was about to make a trip to Colorado to meet with an alumni group. After a further flurry of emails, it was agreed that the president would visit with Mr. Baton during this trip and present him with the approved gift agreement. But when Piccolo contacted Mr. Baton, she learned that he had already left his summer home and was now in the south of France for the next six weeks. "Don't worry," the president's chief-of-staff said when Piccolo delivered this news. "The president can always present the agreement to him some other time."

So much time had now elapsed that Piccolo called a meeting of the college's legal counsel, along with Jim Bass. Everyone shared Piccolo's concerns but had little to offer her in terms of how to speed the process along. Eventually, Mr. Baton's travels came to an end, and he returned to the area. One morning, Piccolo received a phone call from Bass. "The president's going to stop by Mr. Baton's house and have him sign the agreement. Do you want to tag along?" She immediately canceled her next appointments and hurried to the parking lot to join Bass and the president as they set out to meet Mr. Baton.

The meeting started off well, and Mr. Baton even joked about how hard he'd made it for them to track him down. But his mood changed quickly when he read over the gift agreement the president gave him. "What's this? This isn't what we talked about at all."

"Of course, it is," the president replied. "When I was reviewing the agreement with my chief-of-staff, he happened to mention that the marching band's uniforms were only a couple of years old, but the chamber orchestra needed a shell for the auditorium in order to do this summer series they've been planning. You might know my chief-of-staff. His wife's the chair of the chamber orchestra's advisory board. Anyway, I called Jim Bass here, and he mentioned that, in your initial conversation with him, you'd mentioned something about supporting our ensembles. Besides, music's music, right?"

Sara Piccolo sat uncomfortably as Mr. Baton turned to Jim Bass and said, "I thought you understood exactly what I wanted. Aren't you the one who's in charge of this project? This agreement isn't at all what we had in mind. I mean, I'm all for chamber music, but I'm not here in the summer when this series is going to take place. I thought you understood that the cash up front was so that I could see its effect on the marching band in the fall. Besides," and at this point Mr. Baton thumbed through the agreement again, "the only mention of the sheet music, books, and instruments—if it even is a reference—is this clause giving the college the right to sell any tangible property I donate. That wasn't the deal."

Piccolo felt blindsided because none of these changes had been mentioned to her. The president glared at her as though it were her fault that the meeting had taken a bad turn. Piccolo took a deep breath and said, "I think that what's happened is that, in all the time that got away from us since our initial discussions, some wires must have inadvertently been crossed. Let me just apologize for wasting your time this morning. Give us a chance to take this agreement back, re-examine it, and create another draft that better reflects your intent. I'm really sorry all this happened. We'll get back to you just as soon as we can."

The ride back to campus took place in cold silence. When Piccolo followed up the next day, the president's chief-of-staff and Jim Bass seemed completely unfazed by what happened. Bass simply shrugged and said, "Well, you can't win them all," while the chief-of-staff spoke dismissively of Mr. Baton's "weird request."

It became clear to Piccolo that the college's expectation was that she now talk Mr. Baton into accepting the college's version of the gift agreement rather than amending it to better reflect Mr. Baton's intent. Piccolo realized that the prevailing culture at the college was unacceptable to her as a development professional. She met socially with Mr. Baton several weeks later and again apologized for the misunderstanding. Mr. Baton was pleasant about the situation but seemed confused by why he still hadn't received an amended gift agreement. Piccolo decided that she was not going to air the college's dirty laundry and simply deflected the conversation to other topics.

At the end of the academic year, Piccolo resigned her position. The college's development office never contacted Mr. Baton again, and he passed away several years later without leaving anything to the college in his will.

Question: Could an A Team have done anything to create a better outcome?

Case Study Discussion

We might start our discussion of this case study by hoping that Sara Piccolo finds or develops an A Team in her new position because she certainly was stuck with an F Troop at her former job. Jim Bass started off by doing the right thing, precisely what we might expect from an A Team member. He realized that he wasn't the best DO to handle the type of gift Mr. Baton wanted to make, and so he turned the case over to someone who could better meet the donor's needs. But Bass didn't just pass the ball; he left the field immediately afterwards and failed to provide any sort of assistance when his help was later needed.

Even worse, during the ill-fated meeting with Mr. Baton, it became clear that he knew about the changes that had been made to the gift agreement and failed to share them with Piccolo. When that occurred, he was no longer on the same team; in fact, he wasn't even playing the same game.

Everything in this case appears to have been done in a silo. Piccolo drafted the gift agreement. The legal team then reviewed it and probably amended it. The agreement then went to the president's office where, without any further consultation with Piccolo (and apparently without any from the legal team), the chief-of-staff took it upon himself to make further changes, cause unnecessary delays, and give the president bad advice about the donor's likely reaction to those changes.

As the case unfolds, it becomes clear that the chief-of-staff isn't an honest broker: He has a personal interest in those changes because his wife is the chair of the chamber orchestra's advisory board. In a true A Team approach, none of those discussions and revisions would have occurred in isolation. The DO would have presented her draft to the full team, including Bass, the institution's lawyers, the chief-of-staff, and the president.

If she knew that Mr. Baton was about to travel to Colorado and then France, she would have presented those key dates to the group so that they could work out a timetable for their activities. The lawyers would have presented their revisions at a subsequent meeting of the whole group, at which the chief-of-staff could have requested the revisions that he wanted. That would have given Piccolo (and possibly also Bass and the lawyers) an opportunity to suggest why those revisions were inadvisable.

Then, even if the president had insisted that those revisions be made, Piccolo would at least have known about them before the meeting with Mr. Baton. Moreover, she would have known that such a meeting had been scheduled and not had to cancel other appointments and dash out to the parking lot to join a group on the verge of setting out.

The painfulness of this failure probably made a profound impression on Piccolo who would have taken steps to promote an A Team approach in her new job immediately if she discovered that her colleagues were not already following this kind of strategy. If people at her new school wondered why she was so adamant about clear communication and the need to control loose cannons, she now had a compelling anecdote to illustrate the cost of trying to secure a gift otherwise.

CONCLUDING THOUGHTS

In many ways, loose cannons are the antithesis of the A Team approach. While groups are mere collections of individuals and teams are more unified and focused groups, an A Team takes the team approach to the highest possible level. Working with maximum collegial flow (see Chapter 1), members of an A Team know, without being explicitly told, what information other members need and how to make them more effective. (On additional strategies for building unified teams from groups of independent individuals, see Gustavson and Liff, 2014 and Harvey and Drolet, 2005). Loose cannons, however, tend to believe that the rules governing others don't apply to them. They're often so focused on their own responsibilities or careers that they don't give a thought to how the team is judged by the performance of all, not just themselves.

When dealing with a loose cannon, the first thing an A Team tries to do is to educate the person about more effective group fundraising strategies. If that approach doesn't work, they then try to manage the situation so as to mitigate any damage that a loose cannon might do. And if that doesn't work, their last resort is to isolate the loose cannon in some way, either by separating that person from the institution or at least removing the person from any position where he or she might do further harm to the project in question.

REFERENCES

Gustavson, P., & Liff, S. (2014). *A team of leaders: Empowering every member to take ownership, demonstrate initiative, and deliver results*. New York, NY: AMACOM.

Harvey, T. R., & Drolet, B. (2005). *Building teams, building people: Expanding the fifth resource*. (2nd ed.) Lanham, MD: Rowman & Littlefield.

Levine, N. (2016). Private correspondence with authors, dated August 5, 2016.

West, M. (2014) Charitable gifts from wealthy Koch brothers often prompt partisan reactions. *Wall Street Journal*. August 3, 2014, online edition available at www.wsj. com/articles/charitable-gifts-from-wealthy-koch-brothers-often-prompt-partisan-reactions-1407117054.

RESOURCES

Loehr, A., & Kaye, J. (2011). *Managing the unmanageable: How to motivate even the most unruly employee*. Pompton Plains, NJ: Career Press.

Runde, C. E., & Flanagan, T. A. (2008). *Building conflict competent teams*. San Francisco: Jossey-Bass.

Chapter Five

The Team Approach to Working With Volunteers

In *The Department Chair Primer*, Don Chu notes that one of the reasons why academic administrators are sometimes less effective than they'd like to be is that they approach their programs as *closed rather than open systems* (Chu, 2012, 17–19). In a closed system, we only think of the stakeholders who are within the unit itself. Consider, for example, of the typical academic department and how most of the members of that department see themselves (Table 5.1).

It's as though we're seeing the department (or any other academic unit) as sealed inside a box, closed off from the rest of the world (see Figure 5.1.). But viewing a department (or any other academic unit) as a closed system limits its development because this approach fails to take advantage of *all* the stakeholders the program has, such as parents, alumni, the dean, the media, accrediting agencies, professional organizations, and the like. It's far more effective to view an academic unit as an open system with a broad and continually shifting array of stakeholders (see Figure 5.2.).

An A Team isn't likely to make that kind of mistake. It understands that part of its responsibilities includes remaining aware of all its constituents both inside and outside the institution. And one of its most important bridges to that external constituency consists of volunteers and the various boards who advise, assist, or govern the college or university.

Just as we saw in the last chapter that people make philanthropic gifts for a variety of reasons, so do people volunteer their time or serve on boards for several different purposes. Some people view the opportunity to contribute effort to a cause as a natural outgrowth of their philanthropic activities. Others do it for the networking opportunities it provides. Still others do it in order to remain actively involved with something important after they've retired. And there are countless other reasons.

Table 5.1. Self-Image of a Typical Academic Department

Stakeholder Group	Key Function	Members
Constituents	Whose needs do we serve?	Students
Engine	Who does the work?	Faculty
Leadership	Who provides the guidance?	Department Chair
Resources	Who provides space and funding?	Institution

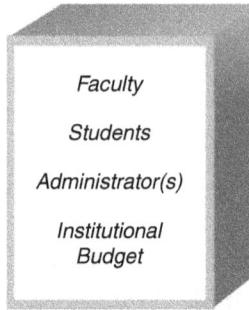

Figure 5.1. An Academic Unit as Closed System.

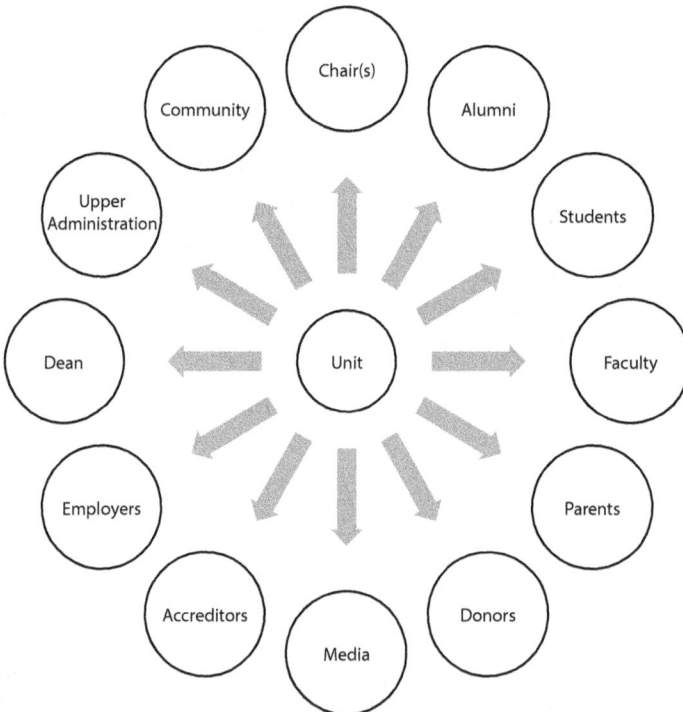

Figure 5.2. An Academic Unit as an Open System.

But volunteers and boards can be either a blessing or a burden to an academic program, depending on how they're organized and the personalities of those involved. For this reason, it's very important for any volunteer group that's working with an A Team to have the right mission, operating procedures, and training. As you probably already know if you've ever worked with volunteers, just keeping a group of people satisfied and moving in a single direction can seem like a never-ending task.

THE VALUE OF VOLUNTEERS AND BOARD SERVICE

We can define volunteerism as the unremunerated donation of time, talent, and/or treasure to a cause with the intention of benefiting others. According to the Independent Sector, a leadership network for non-profits, foundations, and corporate giving programs, the value of volunteer time in 2014 can be estimated at $23.07 per hour, or more than three times the federal minimum wage, at that time (independentsector.org/2014_volunteer_time_release?s=release%20value%20time).

In addition, the U.S. Bureau of Labor Statistics, reports that 25.4% of adult Americans volunteer their time to a cause, with a positive correlation between education level and willingness to volunteer (bls.gov/news.release/volun.nr0.htm). Americans alone volunteered over 8 billion hours of their time in 2013, a contribution that's estimated to be worth over $192 billion (www.volunteeringinamerica.gov/national). In 2014, volunteers spent a median of fifty hours on volunteer activities during the course of the year. So, if, for example, an academic unit at a college or university has twenty advisory board members and as a group they contribute the national median of fifty hours each to the organization, the value of that collective time is $23,070.

That level of participation can make quite a difference in the effectiveness of an organization. And it doesn't even include the ancillary value of volunteers in making introductions to new prospective donors or raising funds through such activities as selling tickets to events or creating products that can then be sold. The advantage of seeing volunteer activity through this financial lens is that it allows the A Team to quantify at least one type of support it receives from the community.

Moreover, in some locations the value of that contribution may be even greater. The value of volunteer time varies widely by state, ranging in 2014 from a low of $19.31 per hour in Arkansas to a high of $39.86 per hour in Washington, D.C. (independentsector.org/uploads/resources/Value-of-Volunteer-Time-by-State-2001-2014.pdf).

Since our focus in this book is academic fundraising for higher education, it's worth noting that, when volunteers calculated the number of hours they gave to their major object of philanthropy, educational or youth-related organizations ranked second only to religious organizations. Perhaps even more interesting, people's level of education played an important role in where they were most likely to volunteer: The more formal education a person had, the greater the probability that he or she would volunteer time to educational or youth-related causes rather than religious causes and activities (www.usnews.com/news/blogs/data-mine/2014/02/26/more-educated-people-do-less-volunteering-for-god).

For this reason, the type of person who's likely to volunteer for a program in higher education is likely to be someone who's attained a relatively high level of formal education and who's willing to contribute a significant amount of time (bls.gov/news.release/volun.nr0.htm).

SELECTING VOLUNTEERS

Volunteers can be invaluable in helping the A Team achieve its goals. No matter how much staffing the institution provides, it's never enough. Volunteers can assist with mailings, website updates, greeting guests at events, hosting lunches for potential donors, and a wide range of other activities. But if you select the wrong volunteers, they can be anything but helpful. They can make your work harder, alienate donors and potential students, and cost you rather than save you money. So, how does an A Team go about choosing which volunteers will be most effective with which types of activities and which volunteers should be politely, but resolutely thanked for their offer but told that there's no opportunity for them to contribute their efforts at this time?

One possibility is to develop a *volunteer screening committee* that meets with each potential volunteer, assesses his or her most valuable form of contribution to the unit, and then recommends a plan of action to the A Team. The volunteer screening committee evaluates each person in terms of the skills and experience he or she would bring the institution, but also in terms of his or her personality, fit, and temperament. Issues for the committee to consider include the following:

- Does the person dominate the conversation to such an extent that others are likely to be alienated by the way he or she interacts with them?

- Does the person appear to be sincerely interested in helping the program, or is this opportunity likely to be just a résumé builder for the person?
- Does the person display any mannerisms that could distract a guest, potential donor, or another volunteer significantly enough to cause a problem?
- Is the person abrasive, demanding, or dismissive toward others?
- Does the person appear to be overly enamored with his or her own ideas?
- Does the person appear to be "high maintenance" to the point that someone from the team will need to devote a great deal of time to addressing his or her needs?

Service on a volunteer screening committee should be reserved for those who represent the qualities the A Team wants in its volunteers: high energy that doesn't overwhelm others, a sincere commitment to the institution, and a canny insight into other people's strengths and weaknesses. If the volunteer screening committee recommends that the A Team decline a person's offer to provide service to the institution, that person's interests can be redirected to other areas, such as making a financial contribution or attending campus events.

The A Team tries never to leave even the most unsuitable volunteer with a negative impression of the institution, but it understands that not everyone is well suited to the type of volunteer work it needs.

ADVISORY BOARDS AND GOVERNING BOARDS

All the reasons why donors participate in philanthropy that we discussed in Chapter 1—social prestige, family tradition, faith, giving back, social interaction, the desire to benefit others, and so on—also apply to volunteers. In fact, volunteers *are* donors. They're merely donating time instead of or in addition to money. These volunteers may serve the institution in a number of ways. They may work independently, serve on an *ad hoc* taskforce such as a presidential search committee, or have a more formal position on a standing body like a council or board.

By understanding each volunteer's motivation for agreeing to serve the institution, the A Team can make better use of that person's talent and interests. One obvious example is that you wouldn't encourage a retired schoolteacher with plenty of time but few resources to serve on a fundraising board where the minimum expected individual contribution is $50,000; that person's efforts are better directed to a community outreach council, a committee that mentors future teachers, or a planning group for an upcoming event. In a similar way, an executive who's long been in charge of *running* an organization may be ill advised to serve on a committee that works very slowly and only proceeds on a plan when all its members agree; that executive would quickly become bored and either grow to be disengaged, annoy the other members of the committee by being too heavy handed, or both.

One overarching requirement is that the volunteer must support the mission and vision of the unit he or she is serving. Just as you wouldn't recruit an ardent atheist to serve on the evangelism committee of a conservative religious college, so should you be careful in appointing someone who views college exclusively as vocational training to work for a liberal arts program in which job preparation is only one part of its mission or goals.

In most cases, the boards associated with higher education institutions are either *advisory boards* or *governing boards*. Other types of boards, such as *leadership boards* and *development boards*, do exist, although most of their functions will be very similar to the two types of boards described below.

Governing boards and advisory boards have one major difference: *The governing board has fiduciary responsibilities and legal liabilities that are defined by its mission; advisory boards don't.* Advisory boards or councils play a number of other roles, including increasing awareness of the academic unit in the community, advocating for and supporting the fundraising activities of the unit, and providing a network of contacts for internships, employment opportunities, and guest speakers. But it doesn't have any legal or financial responsibilities. In this way, the members of an advisory board may *have influence on* the organization's administration, but are not *in charge of* the organization's governance or day-to-day operations.

Perhaps the clearest indicator of this difference is that most governing boards have the power to hire and fire the chief executive officer with whom they work. However, most advisory boards serve at the pleasure of the academic administrators who appointed them.

We can view the major similarities and differences between advisory boards and governing boards in the following way (Table 5.2.).

For another way of outlining the differences between these two types of boards, see Axelrod (2004, 7–8).

Since advisory boards more commonly engage in fundraising than do governing boards, we're going to focus on advisory boards in the pages that follow and explore how the A Team can best work with these groups to advance the mission of their programs. Of course, the first prerequisite for the A Team in this regard is to help create or maintain a "healthy" board.

Table 5.2. Differences Between Advisory and Governing Boards

Advisory Boards	Governing Boards
Do not have legal authority for policy and management	Have legal authority for policy and management
Do not have fiduciary responsibility over assets	Do have fiduciary responsibility over assets
Are not required by law but are established at the discretion of a particular entity	Are required by state law (for many, but not all, types of colleges and universities)
Are generally not personally liable for breach of duty	Are individually liable for breach of duty, although this liability is usually covered by the organization's insurance or indemnification
Are expected to follow ethical guidelines in their official activities	Are required by law to follow ethical guidelines in their official activities
Serve as informal ambassadors and advocates for the entity in order to strengthen its standing in the community	Serve as official ambassadors and advocates for the entity in order to strengthen its standing in the community
Should support the vision and mission of the entity	Determine and thus should support the vision and mission of the entity
Do not determine policy, but may work to create or change policy indirectly	Determine policy and can make decisions in the name of the entity
Do not hire or evaluate administrators or staff	Frequently hire and evaluate the chief administrative officer
Have memberships that are selective, usually determined by the group itself in collaboration with the administration	Have a membership that is selective and may be appointed by a higher governing body (especially for public institutions)
Are expected to directly support fundraising efforts of the unit	Support the organization with financial contributions
May be used as a pathway or "trial run" for consideration to membership on a governing board	Are usually viewed as an end in itself
May or may not have bylaws or guidelines that define roles of members, length of terms, term limits, nomination processes for membership and leadership positions, and member termination procedures	Must have carefully defined bylaws or policies that define roles of members, length of terms, term limits, nomination processes for membership and leadership positions, and member termination procedures
May have a specialized focus, such as fundraising, program review or support, event planning, community engagement, and so on	Have a focus that is governed by bylaws and mission

THE HEALTHY ADVISORY BOARD

Healthy advisory boards aren't necessarily those who agree with the academic officer (AO) or development officer (DO) on every detail. Rather they're those that can work together effectively in order to achieve a common goal. There are ten characteristic features of healthy advisory boards in higher education:

1. *They align their mission and goals so as to support the mission and goals of the academic programs they serve.* As we saw with the development cascade in Chapter 1, each level of the institution has to make sure that its actions and future plans help achieve the goals of the level above it. That principle is particularly true in the case of advisory boards. Since they're composed of people who don't work within the closed system of the college or university, they run the risk of becoming "loose cannons" if they simply pursue the whims of the membership.

   A healthy board needs a mission statement that the members can identify with and use to direct their activities. That mission statement should help drive the board's strategic plan and include a series of specific, written goals with measurable objectives. This mission statement should be printed on the agenda of every meeting or made visible to the members in some other way so that, if the conversation gets off track, it's easier for the chair to refocus the board on its primary purpose.

   BOX 5.1

   One useful practice is to provide board members with business cards, identifying them as volunteers to the institution, college, or program. The board's mission statement can be printed on the back of these cards as a frequent reminder to the members of what they should do and why they're doing it.

   ---

2. *They assist in cultivating external funding to support the program and build the endowment.* Volunteer board members are involved with causes they care about. They should thus be willing to help the A Team develop mutually beneficial relationships with external stakeholders. A significant portion of the members should be willing to ask others to join them in supporting the causes that they themselves support with time and/or financial contributions. A useful way in which the members can do this is by partnering with the A Team on visits to prospects and when they make proposal presentations.

3. *They increase community awareness of the program.* Organizations want community leaders who can help heighten awareness of their programs and attract individuals from various spheres of influence and interaction, both corporate and social. Together, the members of the A Team should strategize how individual board members and other volunteers can best

work "for the cause." For example, some volunteers may want to chair social events, others may want to coordinate interaction with elected officials, and still others may prefer to work behind the scenes.

4. *They ensure that all board activities are ethical and reflect best practices.* The policies and procedures established by the appropriate governing bodies (such as the board of regents or foundation board) should be shared with the advisory board so that everyone is familiar with current practices at the institution. A periodic meeting to train new board members—and to remind current members—of acceptable practices can be invaluable in helping people avoid activities that would create problems for themselves or the school.

   In addition, a key duty assigned to the DO who works with the board should be to take the lead in helping the members understand the development process and the limits that law and ethical standards impose on that process.

5. *They support the board chair and the AO heading the unit they represent.* As we saw earlier, boards that are advisory in nature usually exist at the discretion of the academic leader. The dean, chair, or other administrator can dissolve them at will or dismiss a member for any reason at all. It's important, therefore, for the members of the board to act in ways that don't undermine the goals of the academic leader, development staff, and board chair.

6. *They plan for the smooth transition of their members and officers.* Healthy boards have bylaws or written policies that detail such matters as term limits and the duties expected of their members and officers. These boards teach new members about their duties through formal orientation programs and regular updates that highlight trends in advancement, the local community, and higher education in general.

   Chairs of healthy boards also sometimes attend development conferences or workshops with college administrators and DOs to further develop skills that will, in turn, benefit the entire board.

7. *They support a level of diversity that reflects the community at large.* Advisory boards should look like the stakeholders they serve. For example, if the student body of a school is 50% Caucasian, 25% African-American, 15% Hispanic or Latino, 10% Asian, and 10% other with a 65% female gender imbalance, it'll be difficult to argue that a board consisting solely of retired, white, European-American men can accurately understand all issues that may arise during their time on the board. Diverse boards are more successful at identifying matters of concern to the student body as a whole and avoiding missteps that can make the board seem insensitive or out of touch with the modern university.

8. *They expect that each board member must also be a meaningful donor.* Most academic advisory boards have a fundraising component in their mission. In fact, some of these boards aren't really "advisory" at all; their entire function is to secure external sources of funding. It's difficult for a community member to argue that community financial support is important if he or she hasn't found it important enough to make a contribution.

"Join me in supporting ..." is a far more compelling argument than "Even though I don't, you ought to support ..."

In fact, many boards require their members to make a major gift, no matter how the institution defines that term. But truly large gifts don't have to be made each year. It may be possible to arrange for a pledge to be paid off over several years (even after the member's term has expired) or to take the form of an irrevocable deferred gift.

9. *They refrain from interfering with matters of governance.* One of the most common complaints academic leaders make about advisory boards is that they stray into areas that are beyond their charge. Even though they may be told that their sole concern is with community relations and fundraising, boards sometimes begin to interfere with matters of curriculum, student recruitment, faculty promotion and tenure, grading policies, and other issues beyond their charge.

   Healthy boards avoid this problem. Their mission and vision statements are clear and focused on a defined set of responsibilities. The expectations of members are spelled out in their policies and bylaws. Their chairs are strong enough to redirect discussions when they deviate from the agenda. Although *all* boards seek to work hand-in-glove with the administrative and development team, *healthy* boards develop a working relationship that remains entirely focused on their primary goals, allows for collegial and constructive dissent, and respects the difference between governance bodies and advisory boards.

10. *They are passionate about higher education.* The best advocates for a program are the people who care deeply about it and have some type of personal connection to its aims. They may have been majors in a related discipline themselves. They may work in a similar field. They or a loved one may be facing a problem that is relevant to the focus of the program. Whatever their connection to the discipline might be, the members of healthy boards care deeply about its success. Nothing of significance can be gained without each member's passion for the cause.

THE A TEAM'S ROLE IN DEVELOPING HEALTHY BOARDS

Because the effectiveness of an advisory board can be integral to an academic unit's overall fundraising effort, the A Team will regard it as essential to do everything in its power to ensure that the board is well organized and running smoothly. One useful way of pursuing this goal is to prepare a draft set of bylaws that the board can use to govern its operation. The following template is useful for institutions and units that want to adopt suitable bylaws for an advisory board of volunteers.

ADVISORY BOARD BYLAWS

Latest Revision: [DATE]

Article 1. Members of the [NAME OF UNIT] Advisory Board (hereafter "the Board") are appointed at the discretion of the [CHAIR, DEAN, DIRECTOR, VICE PRESIDENT, PRESIDENT, ETC.] (hereafter "the AO") and serve at this officer's pleasure. The primary administrative contact for members will be the Board's designated "DO." Members are expected to support the following Mission Statement.

The mission of the Board is to

- *Promote community knowledge and awareness of the programs offered by those units that the Board represents.*
- *Develop positive interactions between these programs and the broader community.*
- *Support measures to build the endowment of these programs for scholarships, professorships, programs, and facilities.*
- *Contribute to the Board's Annual Fund and seek to secure additional expendable funding from external sources that can further the work of the Board.*

Article 2. The expectations for members invited to serve on this Advisory Board are as follows:

a. In accordance with the Board's mission statement, members are expected to act as a valuable resource by expanding the institution's endowment for scholarships, professorships, programs and/or facilities by direct giving or by facilitating giving from others.
b. All members will be expected to serve on at least one committee or subcommittee in order to achieve the Board's goals in a timely manner.
c. Members are expected to commit to serving on the Board for at least two years. After their initial two-year term, membership may be renewed for additional two-year terms with the mutual agreement of the AO and the individual member. Members must rotate off the Board for at least one two-year term after having served three consecutive terms (i.e., six years) on the Advisory Board.
d. Members are expected to attend meetings of the Board in order to promote continuity of discussions. In the event a member is unable to attend at least half of these regular meetings, the member may be replaced at the discretion of the AO.

e. Members are expected to attend at least three Board-sponsored events annually in addition to regular meetings.
f. Members are expected to introduce the AO and DO to at least three prospects for cultivation during each two-year term.
g. Members are expected to make an annual contribution to provide support for the discretionary funds of the AO. The minimum amount of this contribution will be set by the AO at the start of each academic year and reviewed annually. This contribution may be paid at any time during the academic year.
h. In addition to the annual gift, each member is to make a substantial gift to the academic programs represented by the Board at least once during his or her tenure on the Board. The size of this gift should be mutually agreed upon by the member and the DO. This gift may be payable over multiple years.

Article 3. The Board should be diverse in its membership. For the purposes of Board membership, diversity shall include matters of gender, race, ethnicity, financial capacity, occupational sector, and relationship to the University (i.e., alumni, parent of existing student, and non-affiliated). Existing members may recommend potential candidates for membership by nominating them to the AO. Current members of the Alumni Society and Parents Council shall be exempt from requirements for financial contributions and committee membership, but are encouraged to participate and support the mission of the Board and the academic units affiliated with it.

Article 4. Board Leadership.

Section A. Chair

Background: The chair is essential to the Board's efficient operation and long-term success. The chair is appointed by the AO for a two-year, non-renewable term. The chair sets the agenda for regular meetings, conducts those meetings, and interacts frequently with the AO and DO to set the goals of the board. The position may be filled by a former chair after at least a one-term hiatus from the position.

Responsibilities: The duties of the Advisory Board Chair include

1. Managing and guiding meetings of the Board in a professional and effective manner.
2. Providing leadership to members of the Board, particularly in the process of decision-making.
3. Appointing committee chairs in consultation with the AO.

4. Working cooperatively with the AO and DO in developing strategies to support the mission of the [NAME OF UNIT] within the areas of the Board's purview.
5. Performing a key fundraising role by providing introductions to, networking with, and promoting interaction among potential donors in close partnership with the AO and DO.
6. Evaluating current Board members and discussing those observations with the AO.
7. Encouraging Board members to consider all perspectives on issues within its purview and helping them achieve consensus whenever possible.
8. Creating opportunities for Board members to learn more about the programs supervised by the AO, successful strategies of community outreach, development, and philanthropy.
9. Representing the [NAME OF UNIT] at appropriate events.
10. Serving *ex officio* as a member of the Steering Committee.

Section B. Vice Chair

Background: The vice chair is appointed by the AO for a two-year term, fulfills the role of chair in his or her absence, and (in most cases) becomes the next chair of the Board.

Responsibilities: The duties of the Advisory Board Vice Chair include

1. Performing the responsibilities of chair when the chair is absent or otherwise unable to perform those duties.
2. Planning for succession in Board leadership.
3. Serving on at least one of the Board's major committees.
4. Serving *ex officio* as a member of the Steering Committee.

Section C. Standing Committees

The Board shall maintain the following standing committees, each of which should meet at least once between regular meetings of the Board, provide written minutes of those meetings for distribution prior to each Board meeting, submit to the Board such items for the consent agenda as may be appropriate, and select a committee chair who shall serve a one-year renewable term.

- *Steering.* Assists the chair with setting the agenda and consent agenda for each meeting. Includes at least one Board member not currently serving as chair, vice chair, or immediate past chair.

- *Community Relations.* Plans community outreach events and submits proposals for such events to the full Board.
- *Corporate Liaison.* Works with businesses in the community to seek possibilities for student internships, financial support, and sponsored programs. Submits names of prospective Board members, derived from these activities, to the Nominating Committee.
- *Nominating Committee.* Proposes to the Academic Officer new prospective Board members and recommends possible chairs and vice chairs for consideration.
- *Government Relations Liaison.* Represents the programs within its purview to elected state and federal officials.
- *Special Events.* Plans at least one major revenue-producing event each year and submits proposals for such events to the full Board.
- *Annual Dinner.* Plans and arranges logistics for an annual dinner for members, spouses of members, prospective members, and invited members of the community.
- *Planned Giving.* Advises the AO and DO about policies related to planned giving activities, recommends potential donors, and (in close consultation with the AO and DO) assists in the cultivation of such donors.

Section D. Ad Hoc Committees and Taskforces.

From time to time the Board, AO, or DO shall appoint ad hoc committees or taskforces to undertake specific tasks. Unless other provisions are made, these ad hoc committees or taskforces shall disband one year after their creation or when their charge is complete, whichever comes first.

DISCUSSION OF THE BYLAWS TEMPLATE

Every A Team will want to make adjustments to this template so that it reflects the distinctive nature of the academic programs served by the advisory board. Some of these adjustments will be merely stylistic. For example, you may prefer to retain certain terms like *dean* or *department chair* throughout the document instead of adopting the sometimes cumbersome expression AO. Additionally, you may prefer slightly longer or shorter terms for officers on the board or wish to replace some of the recommended committees with others more germane to the needs of the academic unit. But other aspects of these bylaws should be changed only after careful consideration.

For example, it's important for the board members to serve at the pleasure of the AO. While it doesn't happen often, there are times when a particular member proves so detrimental to the successful operation of the board that it's undesirable to let the problem fester until his or her term expires.

In addition, it's highly destructive to have a situation in which a board member is undermining or openly opposing the policies of the AO. Including a clause that indicates the president, provost, dean, or chair has the authority to drop a member from the board at any time, without even providing a reason, is a good precaution against these problems.

In a similar way, it's important to spell out precisely where the Board's role begins—and where it ends. As we saw earlier, some Boards attempt to advise or even develop policies on matters that are far outside their intended function. Having that function specified in the bylaws provides protection against this type of mission creep. Imposing term limits is another way you can discreetly remove unsuccessful members from the Board.

Without such limits, it can be awkward to end the position of a member who, while well intentioned, isn't really achieving the goals you've set. No matter how kindly you phrase your remarks, the member is likely to feel as though he or she has been "fired" from the Board, and in some ways that's exactly what's happened. Term limits avoid these difficult situations. When the person's term is over, you don't have to remove that member from the Board; the bylaws do it for you.

The same advantage occurs with the "sunset policy" about *ad hoc* committees and taskforces. Groups that are created for a single purpose occasionally want to continue to work together, even though the reason for its existence has already been achieved. Having a rule that automatically disbands them saves you from the uncomfortable task of actively dissolving them, thus potentially causing hard feelings among a group of valued supporters. In sum, well-conceived bylaws for the advisory board help you create an expanded A Team that includes, not merely members of the paid staff, but also highly motivated volunteers from the community.

ELECTION VERSUS APPOINTMENT ON ADVISORY BOARDS

Because of the way most boards and committees work in higher education, there's a great temptation to have officers selected by the means commonly used by other college and university groups: election. In fact, electing the chair, vice chair, and other officers can be a very empowering activity for the board—as long as you'd be happy with anyone they select and have reason to believe that all future board members will be equally effective in a leadership role if they're ever chosen.

The fact remains, however, that even on healthy boards, not every member would make an effective officer. If the wrong person is elected, you can have a real problem on your hands. You'll either have to wait out that person's term (in the meantime enduring any damage the person might cause) or have an awkward situation in which you have to remove a duly elected officer.

The best solution is thus to establish the board from the beginning in a way that permits the AO to select all board officers. Deans and department chairs are sometimes reluctant to adopt such a policy. They ask, "Won't it bother the members if they're simply told who their officers are and have no voice in that decision? Won't I offend someone who wants to be an officer but is consistently overlooked?" But the fact is that most board members look at the selection of officers in a completely different way from how faculty members view committee chairs.

Board members typically come from corporate or professional environments where supervisors are chosen all the time without consultation of the people being supervised. They're used to that practice. Moreover, you'll frequently find that the very same person who's secretly yearning to be chosen as an officer is the member that you (and probably most of his or her colleagues on the board) would least want in a leadership role.

The selection of advisory board officers is one of those activities for which democracy is usually not the best choice. Board leadership shouldn't be a popularity contest; it should be a reflection of your own views about effective supervision of board meetings and activities.

ORIENTATION OF NEW ADVISORY BOARD MEMBERS

It's always a good idea to provide formal orientation for new advisory board members. The program can be relatively brief—members of the board frequently have important responsibilities at their job or on other boards, and an A Team always respects their time—but it should highlight the mission and vision of the academic unit itself and the board, the duties of board members, and the role members are expected to play at meetings. In order to provide a few ideas, here's a sample agenda for the orientation of an academic advisory board:

- Welcome by the AO, DO, and board chair.
- Self-introductions of the new members.
- Introductions of academic leaders with whom the Board works closely.
- Introductions of the DO's staff.
- Brief overview of the institution (if the Board serves a particular unit of the institution and not the institution as a whole).

- Brief introduction to the academic unit's mission, vision, guiding principles, and recent activities.
- Discussion of duties and expectations for board members.
- Overview of the fundraising process at the institution and the Board's fundraising priorities.
- List of annual events and special initiatives in which members traditionally participate.
- Brief student presentations, if possible.

The last item on the agenda may require some explanation. It's highly desirable to end the orientation by having the new members meet some of the students who benefit from board activities. This part of the orientation helps the members put a face on activities that can occasionally seem onerous or remote from the central mission of the academic unit.

Besides, orientations necessarily convey a great deal of information. They can seem dry and uninspiring unless enlivened in some way that leaves the new members energized about what they'll be doing. If the members truly care about higher education (as all board members should), they'll find the students' stories interesting and inspiring, causing the orientation to end on a very positive note.

EVALUATION OF ADVISORY BOARD MEMBERS

In addition to effective bylaws, healthy advisory boards should have regular systems in place for evaluating their members. Even though the board may have term limits, some members may adopt the attitude that "I've done my work. Now let someone else carry the load." That type of mindset can be so destructive that it may be unwise to wait until the member's term limit is reached.

A well-conducted evaluation by the AO, with assistance from the DO, can help the member either jumpstart his or her enthusiasm or consider withdrawing from the board. It may even be possible that the evaluation will lead the person to consider some other role that would support the academic unit through a different approach or have different responsibilities.

The most effective types of board evaluations provide at last three perspectives:

1. How the member views his or her own contribution to the board.
2. How the AO views that role.
3. How the development staff views that role.

In the best case scenario, all three of these evaluations will align and indicate that the member is indeed performing valuable service to the board. The warning signs are when one evaluation differs radically from the other two, all three of the evaluations are distinctly different, or the evaluations agree but suggest that the member's work on the board has not met expectations.

The appearance of one of these warning signs shouldn't immediately be taken as a reason for terminating that member's service to the board. Rather it should be used as an opportunity to begin a dialogue about how the member views his or her responsibilities and what might be done to bring that view closer to the expectations of the AO and DO. For certain boards, two other sources of information will also be valuable.

4. How the other members of the board view the member's contribution.
5. How the other members of the A Team view the member's contribution.

Not all boards are strong enough to be able to withstand the criticism of one member by his or her peers. But in cases where the members are strong enough to take what can sometimes be rather bitter medicine, peer-to-peer evaluations can be very revealing and eliminate any perception that negative observations are due merely to a personality conflict between the AO and the member. Insights from the other members of the A Team can also be valuable.

For example, a board member might be polite and constructive when addressing the president or a dean, but dismissive when dealing with students, alumni, or staff members. Having these additional perspectives helps develop a more complete view of the member's strengths and weaknesses.

A template for a possible board member evaluation form appears below. While this template is presented in the form of a self-evaluation, it can easily be adapted for use by the AO, DO, or other reviewers. One unexpected outcome of this evaluation process is that board members may sometimes think they're not doing enough in their current role, while the AOs or DOs are well satisfied with the person's contribution. Subsequent conversations can thus be used to assuage the member's fears and provide reassurance that the institution is well satisfied with what the member is doing.

More commonly, however, there will be members who will rank themselves very highly even though others don't share this opinion. In this case, the evaluation process provides an opportunity for a tactful reappraisal of the expectations for board members, the level of commitment that others have, and the possibility that board membership is not the right "fit" for this particular individual.

ACADEMIC ADVISORY BOARD

Member Self-Evaluation Form

INSTRUCTIONS: This form provides us with a tool we can use together to help determine your level of commitment to the Academic Advisory Board. When you have completed the form, please submit it to the board liaison. The board liaison will then contact you and schedule an appointment to discuss your position and/or any concerns.

KEY: Unless the question states otherwise, please use the following system to score yourself.

Excellent: 5; Very Good: 4; Fair: 3; Could do better: 2; Nothing to report here at all: 1

FOCUS   SCORE

1. Attends Board meetings (one point per meeting to max of 5 points) _____
2. Participates in Board meetings (i.e., joins discussions, adds insight) _____
3. Understands expectations of board members _____
4. Is an active committee member (if a chair position, score the full 5 points) _____
5. Has passion for the mission of the academic programs _____
6. Invites the Academic Officer/faculty/students to *non-Board* events _____
7. Can name individual professors (one point per name) _____
8. Advocates for the academic programs in other settings _____
9. Encourages excellence in all Board activities _____
10. Attends standing Board events and activities _____
11. Attends special (i.e., non-standing) Board events and activities _____
12. Attends fundraising events, etc. (one point for each event to a max of 5 points) _____
13. Introduces new individuals to the institution to expand awareness (one point per person to a max of 5 points) _____
14. Makes solicitation calls with the Academic Officer or Development Officer _____
15. Leverages multiple board positions to benefit the academic programs _____
16. Initiates approaches or discusses concerns with academic leadership _____

17. Sponsored at least one event in the past year _____
18. Has endowed a scholarship or program (2 points per $10K; max 5 pts) _____
19. Hosted a luncheon or dinner to facilitate interaction between the institution and community leaders _____
20. Facilitated a major gift from an employer _____

TOTAL POINTS _____

BOX 5.2 SCORE YOURSELF!

70 and Above	Outstanding! You are a leader in the success of our academic programs!
60–69	Your dedication is evident and greatly benefits faculty and students.
40–59	Your participation is truly appreciated; we would like to see more of you!
25–39	Let's talk about how our interaction can be mutually more rewarding.
Below 24	Perhaps another role for you or another time for your Board membership is something we should discuss.

CASE STUDY

A college has an advisory board that initially was quite productive but recently has stagnated and seems to have lost its direction. The focal point of most members' discontent is one recent addition to the group who consistently sidetracks discussions at regular meetings by mentioning irrelevant topics, proposes activities for the group that either aren't feasible or would require far too great an investment relative to their payoff, and loudly shoots down most ideas proposed by other members.

Currently the board is suffering from a particularly weak chair who happens to be the same person who introduced the problematic new member to the board. Meetings have become so unproductive and disagreeable that several very active board members have asked to step down, and the dean fears that the entire board may be on the verge of collapse. The dean meets with his DO and discusses several options:

1. They could simply force the troublesome member off the board since everyone in the group "serves at the pleasure of the dean," according to the bylaws.
2. They could replace the ineffective chair with someone who can lead the meetings with a stronger hand.
3. They could have candid talks with the member, the chair, or both.
4. They could dissolve the entire board since it hasn't been productive recently, devote a period of time to developing a new set of bylaws, and establish a new advisory board in a year or two.

5. They could simply wait out the term of the current chair and the difficult board member, both of whom have only one more year in their term (although the bylaws state that each could be renewed).
6. They could try something else.

Since the advisory board is an important aspect of the college's community engagement activity, the dean and DO would like to solve this problem without offending people unnecessarily.

Questions

1. Based only on what you know so far, what advice would you give to the dean and DO?
2. The case study did not contain any pronouns indicating the gender of either the member or the chair. Which genders did you visualize? Would you respond any differently if one or both were not the gender you'd imagined?
3. What if the problematic member was the sole representative of a racial or ethnic minority on the board, and the college had long had great difficulty in attaining even this level of diversity? What if the chair were the sole member of that racial or ethnic minority? What if both were the only two members of the board who represented that particular racial or ethnic minority?
4. What if the chair or the member was particularly sensitive and tended to have his or her feelings hurt easily?
5. What if the member were the college's largest donor?
6. What if the member or the chair were the spouse of the institution's president?

Possible Strategies

This problem is one that should be approached with a "minimally invasive" strategy. In other words, from an advancement viewpoint, a priority has to be placed on maintaining strong relationships with members of the board. Although a total dissolution of the board would probably be effective in establishing new ground rules, it almost certainly would alienate some long-term supporters, and the cost of this approach could be high. It's probably best to begin with a relaxed, informal meeting with the board chair and the problematic member.

If the problem is severe enough, an "honest broker," such as a consultant or mediator, might be brought in to see if a solution can be found that suits the needs of all parties. The rationale for taking this step would be the A Team's expressed desire to strengthen the board and keep it focused on its mission. As an added advantage, the external party can take the pressure off of the dean and DO by accepting the "blame" for any hard choices that need to be made. Best of all, if the consultant works with the entire board to improve its operations, there will be more benefits that result than just a solution to the immediate problem.

However the issue is approached, it should be regarded as a "teachable moment." After all, there really are two problems here: a weak chair and a troublesome board member. By meeting with the chair, the dean can help develop some strategies that can be used to keep the meetings on track and avoid the problem of any one member dominating the discussions. The dean can use this opportunity to help the chair grow in his or her leadership role, thus providing a useful service at the same time that the problem at hand is being addressed.

CONCLUDING THOUGHTS

Working with volunteers can be one of the most rewarding and challenging aspects of fundraising. Volunteers bring academic units fresh perspectives, new energy, and (of course) free labor. But volunteers can also create problems for your fundraising efforts.

For example, they may say that they'll arrive to assist with an event, but then fail to show. They may pledge a certain level of financial support, but fail to honor their pledge.

They may propose interesting new ideas at meetings of an advisory board, but then expect the institution to provide all the funding and labor needed to make those ideas a reality. Organizing volunteers into formal units, such as advisory or development boards, which have official bylaws and operating procedures will reduce but cannot eliminate these problems.

Even so, however, the most active members of a healthy advisory board can become valuable members of your A Team, helping to reinforce the notion that your college or university is an open rather than a closed system. For more on what members of an A Team need to know about working with volunteers, see the Volunteer Involvement section of the Certified Fund Raising Executive (CFRE) Examination Content Outline in Appendix III.

REFERENCES

Axelrod, N. R. (2004). *Advisory councils*. Washington, DC: BoardSource.
Chu, D. (2012). *The department chair primer: Leading and managing academic departments*. (2nd Ed.) San Francisco, CA: Jossey-Bass.

RESOURCES

Gifford, G. L. (2012). *How to make your board dramatically more effective, start-ing today: A board member's guide to asking the right questions.* Medfield, MA: Emerson & Church.

Grace, K. S. (2008). *The ultimate board member's book: A 1-hour guide to under-standing and fulfilling your role and responsibilities.* Medfield, MA: Emerson & Church.

Greenfield, J. M. (2008). *Fundraising responsibilities of nonprofit boards.* Washington, DC: BoardSource.

Ingraham, Richard T. (2009). *Ten basic responsibilities of nonprofit boards.* (2nd Ed.). Washington, DC: BoardSource.

Lansdowne, D. (2000). *Fund raising realities every board member must face: A 1-hour crash course on raising major gifts for nonprofit organizations.* Medfield, MA: Emerson & Church.

Zimmerman, R. M., & Lehman, A. W. (2004). *Boards that love fundraising: A how-to guide for your board.* San Francisco, CA: Jossey-Bass.

Chapter Six

Taking an Existing Team to the Next Level

One of the authors' favorite cartoons when they were children was *Goofus and Gallant*, the ongoing series about courtesy and good behavior that Garry Cleveland Myers and Anni Matsick created for the magazine *Highlights for Children*. In each situation, Goofus would demonstrate the wrong way to behave while Gallant was a model of etiquette and thoughtfulness. F Teams and A Troops are a lot like Goofus and Gallant. While F Troops provide us with negative examples, the success of A Teams provides us with plenty of models of excellent practices to imitate.

In the real world, however, not everyone is either a Goofus or a Gallant, a member of either an F Troop or an A Team. Judging from our own experience, we've found that the world is full of B, C, and D Squads as well. So, in this final chapter we want to ask what people can do if they're already part of an academic development team but not yet achieving the level of A Team success that they'd like. How, in short, can readers apply the lessons they've encountered throughout this book so as to increase their effectiveness at academic fundraising?

We'll begin by returning to an idea we first encountered in Chapter 1: the distinction between an A Team's core and ancillary members. The core of an A Team, as you'll recall, consists of an academic officer (AO) and a development officer (DO). The ancillary members might include anyone who can contribute meaningfully either to one specific project or a series of related projects. Typical ancillary members might be additional academic representatives (such as deans, department chairs, and faculty members), additional representatives from the office of development (such as the vice president (VP), other DOs, and support staff members), and people with the expertise or perspective needed in order to achieve the goals established by the core members.

Core members of an A Team need to meet frequently. At least an hour a week is required for them to develop the ease of communication necessary for their success. In these regular meetings, the AO can establish or reinforce the long-term and immediate needs the academic area has in fundraising; and the DO can outline or reiterate the primary strategies that would be necessary to fill those needs.

In addition, the core team should get together several times a year for more extensive training. On their own, the members of this core team can work on projects like practicing their storytelling techniques in a mini-retreat or extended workshop like the one described in Chapter 6 of the companion volume to this book, *Going for the Gold: How to Become a World-Class Academic Fundraiser* (2016).

They can go to conferences such as those sponsored by the Council for Advancement and Support of Education (CASE). CASE meetings are particularly useful opportunities for obtaining additional training and keeping the members' skills sharp. The AO and DO can attend various sessions, and then meet together in the evening or between presentations to discuss how the concepts introduced in these sessions apply to their current projects.

Although ancillary members don't need to meet as often as the core members, they do need to get together periodically to discuss strategies and make sure that everyone is on the same page. The worst scenario occurs when the full team assembles only when meeting with a prospective donor. When that happens, the chances for miscommunication and muddled strategies increases tremendously.

At the very least, there should be a planning session before meeting with a prospect in which the members discuss explicitly what each of their roles will be, who will say what, when various ideas will be introduced, and how they can communicate subtly among themselves if a situation starts to move in an unanticipated manner. Obviously, no meeting with a donor ever can—or should—be scripted down to the last detail.

The unexpected will always occur, and while an A Team can plan what each of its members will say, it can't predict what the donor may say. For this reason, the practice meeting always involves a mere outline of responsibilities for the members and the points they will raise. Being too scripted can actually work against a group when a prospective donor doesn't react as predicted.

BOX 6.1

An A Team always expects that a meeting with a prospect will unfold more like improvisational comedy than a fully scripted play.

While these planning sessions are essential to an A Team's success, it's far better if the core and ancillary members meet more often than on that single occasion. When people get to know one another, they learn more about each other's strengths and weaknesses, as well as how people will respond to different situations.

For example, in Chapter 4, we explored a case study in which a college president was married to the executive director of a women's health center. If the group knew that the president was likely to respond unfavorably when a donor spoke dismissively about issues of concern to women, other members could have been more proactive in guiding the conversation away from this sensitive subject or swiftly intervening in the conversation before the president said something that would derail the cultivation effort.

THE VALUE OF F TROOPS

Even though it can be frustrating in the extreme to work with an F Troop, these dysfunctional fundraising teams do serve one important purpose: They illustrate for us all the things that we shouldn't do. Even better, they illustrate for us *why* we shouldn't do those things. The authors will never stop being grateful to all the wonderful mentors and role models whom they encountered during their careers in academic fundraising.

But as perverse as it sounds, they're grateful, too, to all the terrible academic fundraisers out there (and there are a surprising lot of them) who provide A Teams with a continuing education course in what not to do. Here is just a sampling of the lessons people can learn from F Troops that can help them improve their success in academic development:

- *F Troops don't do their homework.* As a result, they end up saying the wrong thing at the wrong time, missing opportunities, and becoming blindsided by situations they could easily have predicted.
- *F Troops don't communicate well with one another or the rest of the institution.* They see others as competitors rather than partners in a common enterprise. By withholding information from others, they set an example that it's okay to withhold information from them, and so they end up making mistakes that a little teamwork could have avoided.
- *F Troops don't get back to people.* They see themselves as so busy that they don't have the time to answer all their phone calls and emails. They thus send a message to donors that they're not important, and they treat their colleagues as though their questions and needs are not a priority.
- *F Troops rest on their laurels.* If a particular strategy worked in the past, they keep using it despite its diminishing returns. They don't understand

the need to have a lot of different tools in their toolbox because every challenge they face is going to be different.

• *F Troops see their loyalty as to the institution only, not to both the institution and the donor*. As a result, they leave donors with a sense that they've
been used and frequently try to press prospects to agree to contributions
that aren't a good fit for their philanthropic interests.

• *F Troops don't see the big picture*. They take everything people say at
face value, not realizing that donors (and frankly many university administrators as well) sometimes make grandiose declarations for rhetorical
purposes and don't assume that others will take them literally. They don't
have a good sense of the difference between a statement made for dramatic
effect and one that comes from the heart.

• *F Troops don't take full advantage of the fact that fundraising is a team
activity*. When a member of an F Troop gets in over his or her head during
a complex discussion, he or she doesn't reach out to others who may have
dealt with that situation before or have better training in that area. Members
of an F Troop try to fix things on their own, too often making a problem
worse rather than solving it.

The usefulness of F Troops in teaching us to avoid these poor practices
helps explain why the authors devoted so much attention to them in this book.
Sometimes it's hard to learn how to improve your tennis from world-class
players or how to lead your organization better by seeing what the founders
of Fortune 500 companies did.

Particularly when you're just starting out, it's not easy to imitate people
who are already at the top of their game. So, for people who are just getting a start in academic fundraising, are new to an institution, or just not
satisfied with their rate of success so far, A Teams can be a bit intimidating
at times. "Sure, *they* can do it," someone might think, "but they've got
years of experience and this incredible rapport with one another that we
can't be expected to have yet." But anyone can learn from an F Troop. We
learn from their mistakes. They create problems *so that we don't have to*.
We watch where they go wrong, and then we know precisely which path
to avoid.

THE NEED FOR SIMPLICITY

Successful academic fundraising requires what is known as *boundary spanning*: the ability to translate ideas generated by a group with a particular
vocabulary, set of assumptions, and way of looking at the world to other
groups that have different vocabularies, assumptions, and ways of looking

at the world. A Teams become very proficient at boundary spanning because they have to engage in it all the time.

The academic members of the team come to discussions with one set of priorities and perspectives while the development members of the team come to those discussions with another set. When the core members are augmented with representatives from athletics, marketing, alumni affairs, and other divisions of the institution, they have to take the mind set of those other areas into account as well. The skill they develop in describing concepts in ways that people who are different from them can understand is a big part of the A Team's success.

If a prospective donor is motivated by a desire for prestige, they can address that need. If the donor is more concerned about tax advantages or bringing about lasting social change, they can speak to those needs. In fact, all the different reasons why people engage in philanthropy that we considered in Chapter 1 are familiar to the A Team, and its members are comfortable translating how a given project might relate to those reasons.

An important skill that A Teams develop—and that serves to differentiate them from less effective fundraising teams—is the ability to boil complex concepts down to their essence and present them in a simple and compelling manner. A donor may be very interested in naming an endowed faculty position but become bored with the details of distinguishing salary from benefits, start-up funds from continuing investments, the precise nature of the trust that's established, and all the other details that go into making one of these gifts a reality. So, members of an A Team look for ways to convey the essence of an idea without getting sidetracked by less important matters.

Think, for example, of how we have tried to introduce various concepts throughout this book:

- The Three Ds.
- The Three Ps.
- The STARS Approach.
- The Denny's Grand Slam Approach.

Each of these four mnemonic devices was developed in an effort to simplify principles that may otherwise have been too buried in detail to have been immediately useful to the reader. In much the same way, A Teams can refine ideas that an F Troop might prefer to complicate and express them in language that resonates with the audience.

If you haven't had much practice clarifying ideas before, consider engaging in the following exercise with your academic advancement team. Start by taking any complex project that you're currently working on and say, "There are really only three things you need to know about" whatever the project is. Have each member of the team jot down his or her own concept of what those three things might be before sharing that list with the rest of the group.

As an A Team coalesces over time, those lists will become more and more identical until finally everyone immediately finds the same three aspects of a project to be the most important things a prospective donor needs to know. And if you find an interesting way to turn that list of important ideas into an acronym or other mnemonic device, so much the better.

THE CHALLENGE OF COMPLEXITY

Even though there are great advantages in keeping most matters as simple as possible, there are also times in academic fundraising when simplicity just isn't possible. Certain gifts are going to require knowledge of federal and state tax laws, accepted accounting procedures, business law, international finance, and contract requirements. Members of an A Team are well trained in their own areas of specialty. They're also broadly cross-trained so that they can better understand each other's responsibilities and fill in for one another when necessary. But they also know their limits. They know better than to express an opinion on a complex legal or financial matter that they "think" is correct without getting the best professional advice of specialists.

Often these specialists become ancillary members of the A Team because they provide skills that the other members of the team lack. One way of thinking of an A Team, therefore, is that it *consists of the full complement of specialists needed to handle each assignment together as a seamless unit with professionalism and efficiency, focusing their attention on a shared goal.*

THE IMPORTANCE OF CLEAR PROCEDURES

In homogeneous work groups, there's much that can be accomplished without the need to write down every step the members of those groups take. For example, on the academic side of the institution, almost everyone knows the steps you have to go through to get a new course approved, have a faculty member's credentials certified, or waive a degree requirement.

Among DOs, it's usually taken for granted that people know how to book a gift, seek approval for using restricted funds for a purpose other than the one specified in the gift agreement, and secure naming rights for a facility. But in a cross-functional team like the one we've been discussing in this book, a lot more needs to be spelled out. A faculty member might assume that, simply because a donor contributed $100,000 for equipment and $25,000 for supplies, it's not a big deal to spend some of the equipment money on supplies if the need arises.

Conversely, a DO might not think there's anything wrong with telling a donor that, in return for a gift of a certain size, a new course of the donor's choosing can be added to the curriculum. When we complicate this situation further by thinking of all the rules that might govern such areas as athletics, marketing, and student affairs, it's easy to see that the diversity of an A Team can become one of its greatest liabilities if policies aren't established about who can approve what and under which circumstances.

To a certain extent, many of the procedures adopted by an A Team will flow directly from the group's understanding of sound ethical practices of fundraising, like those described in Chapter 2 of the companion volume to this book, *Going for the Gold: How to Become a World-Class Academic Fundraiser* (2016). The principles of ethical fundraising help ensure that the group's focus is always on the best interests of the donors as well as the institution and that no one is tempted to cut corners improperly in order to secure a gift.

But in addition to these standard good practices of fundraising, the test runs of strategies that an A Team conducts at its periodic meetings serve as a mechanism for clarifying procedures to members of the group before a mistake is made. It allows representatives from athletics to say things like, "But if we let the student-athletes keep those laptops, that would constitute an inappropriate payment or gift." and representatives from public relations to express concerns like, "On what data are you basing your claim that the program is currently the fastest growing in our region? We can't publish a statement of that sort without the facts to back it up."

In instances like these, it's unlikely that the A Team will actually write a new policy or amend its operating procedures. But by doing an oral test run of what will happen during an upcoming meeting or campaign, the members of the team have an opportunity to critique what other members will do and thus clarify standard operating procedures in their areas.

THE POWER OF STORIES

In *Going for the Gold* (2016), we discussed how important it was for members of an academic fundraising team to be able to listen to and tell stories effectively. But notice, too, how integral stories were to the ideas explored in this book: We repeatedly used case studies to illustrate and expand on the various principles that we explored. That's because A Teams improve their skills by learning from their own stories (capitalizing on their successes and understanding their mistakes), listen to the stories of other team members in order to get to know them better, become well versed in the life stories of their donors and prospects, and seek to become adept in telling their institution's story.

No one will deny that academic fundraising requires a breadth of knowledge and skills—see, for example, Appendix III for a summary of what certified fundraising executives are supposed to know—but an intellectual mastery of this material isn't enough. Successful fundraising requires extraordinary people skills and the ability to make ideas come alive for others. People need to see the future in order to want to build it. And becoming proficient at listening to and telling stories is an essential part of making those ideas come alive.

For this reason, an A Team devotes a great deal of energy to improving its storytelling techniques. Its members can tell the stories of the institution and its programs effortlessly and in a way that causes the listener to understand why the team is excited to be associated with such an opportunity.

For every cause they support, they can tell the stories of people who were helped by it or could potentially benefit from it if only additional funding existed. They're particularly adept at success stories, celebrating the triumphs of the school's students and faculty in such a way that those listening to the story will want to become part of this winning team. In fact, that's the primary reason why A Teams and storytelling go so well together. Each story becomes an invitation to "join our team" and, because the group knows one another so well and works together so effortlessly, they convey the spirit of a true team, not just a random assortment of employees who are trying to get the prospect to make a contribution.

THE ROLE OF FIT

Since members of an A Team see themselves as working on behalf of both the institution where they work and the donors who support that institution, they're always concerned that there's a good fit between the institution's needs and the donor's philanthropic goals. In Chapter 3, we saw what happens when fundraising strategies don't align with the mission of the program pursuing them. But a lack of fit can also occur in other ways.

Accepting a gift that is of no real benefit to the institution is poor fundraising practice. It can even be detrimental to the school if it becomes necessary to divert funds from other projects in order to insure, maintain, or manage the gift.

Conversely, cajoling a donor into supporting a program that he or she doesn't really believe in is shortsighted. The immediate gain from the gift is more than outweighed by the bad feelings this type of manipulation can cause and the likelihood that this donor won't make any further gifts to the institution in the future. He or she may even dissuade other potential donors from making a contribution. So, paying close attention to fit isn't just a matter of being ethical; it's also the key to effective and practical fundraising.

Finding the right fit for a donor and the institution can sometimes require a bit of creativity. But when the right match is found, the result can be magical. That's what happens in our next scenario, the final case that we'll consider in this book.

CASE STUDY

How does an A Team measure its success? There are a lot of metrics one can use: proposals submitted, donors visited, funding received in various categories (expendable, endowment, restricted endowment, pledged, bequests, and the like), attendance at events, increases over the previous year, new prospects cultivated, and many other traditional measurements that DOs track regularly.

But there's one factor that tells an A Team that it's truly reached the level of success that distinguishes it from its peers: when other teams begin to imitate it. As the English author Charles Caleb Colton first said in 1820, "Imitation is the sincerest [form] of flattery." A Teams know they're being effective when they find that their approaches have been imitated.

A self-made businessman whom we'll call Benjamin Fredericks was gradually moving away from active involvement in the day-to-day operation of his company and leaving it in the hands of his children. He credited his immense financial success to two factors: his education and the philanthropy of others that helped him receive that education.

Fredericks had grown up in a very poor family. He worked odd jobs throughout college to help pay for housing and food, but even those sources weren't enough. Despite earning a 3.5 Grade Point Average (GPA), he was on the verge of having to drop out when an anonymous benefactor supplied the funds that allowed him to continue and eventually graduate. "I never knew who that person was," Fredericks said, "but I was always grateful. Without that donor, I wouldn't have had any of the success that came later."

Inspired by this example, Fredericks later began to help those in need with anonymous gifts that he called his "random acts of kindness." The DO of a university near where he retired heard about what Fredericks was doing through a mutual friend and approached him about the possibility of making these "random acts" a little more systematic.

At first Fredericks was only interested in making a few small gifts. He supplied some modest amounts to students with severe financial need but good academic records and believed he was now doing for others what that anonymous benefactor had once done for him. As a regular donor, Fredericks was assigned an A Team that provided ongoing stewardship: Students who received the scholarship support would write letters of gratitude to their anonymous donor, and the DO, a dean, and at times the university's president would meet with him to review the letters.

Fredericks was touched by what he read in the letters, but he still felt that one thing was missing. "I need the students to understand that this education will give them opportunities they wouldn't have otherwise. But those opportunities come with their own moral obligation: They need to help others someday and see that this process of each generation helping the next keeps moving forward."

The DO nodded in understanding, "You want them to know that they have a moral obligation to pay it back."

"I think," the dean said, "Mr. Fredericks is talking about a moral obligation to pay it *forward*."

The philanthropist immediately warmed to the idea. Initially his concept was that each fellowship would be a loan, which the students would have thirty years to repay. In that way, the fund would never be depleted and could continue forever.

But the DO pointed out the problems with such an idea. Loans were governed by a complex set of regulations that the university's development office wasn't sufficiently staffed to implement. "Besides, what would happen if the student had a crisis and *couldn't* pay back the loan? Would there be collateral? Would the person be made to feel like a failure? I don't think that's what you want. You yourself used the expression *moral obligation*. Let's build the program from that basis."

Over the next few months, the A Team worked with Fredericks to clarify the details of what would come to be the Fredericks Pay It Forward Scholarship. The application for the scholarship would include a letter from Fredericks telling his personal story and urging the recipients to reach out and give a helping hand to others during their lifetime.

The form included a brief section stating that the applicants understood that they had benefited from an act of kindness and that, over thirty years, they would contribute at least as much to the university as they had received, *if such gifts were financially possible*. To underscore the importance of this provision, the students would have to sign that section separately from their signature on the entire application.

Not having tried anything of this sort before, the members of the A Team had some apprehension as to whether or not students would want to participate in such a program. To their delight, dozens of students applied for this new program as soon as it was launched. Rather than being put off by the idea of a scholarship that came with a moral obligation, they embraced the idea. Fredericks was so pleased that he increased the funding for the program after a year.

Within two years, the DO received the first call among many that would soon follow. It was from the development office of another university that had heard about the program and wanted to set up one like it. By the time the program was five years old, the members of the A Team had lost count of the number of schools—including, to their immense delight, Fredericks' own alma mater—who had contacted them about how to start a Pay It Forward Scholarship. "We should have franchised it like McDonalds," the dean said when yet another such request was received.

"No," Fredericks replied. "I think by telling other schools how to set up this kind of program, you're really just paying it forward, too."

CONCLUDING THOUGHTS

A Teams may be born of necessity, but they mature due to their sheer effectiveness. Fundraising in higher education today is so complicated that no one can possibly master every aspect of it. The team approach works because each member contributes his or her own expertise and does so in a highly coordinated manner.

Members of an A Team differ in their backgrounds, training, and areas of specialty, but they're united in working toward the same goal. As we saw at the very beginning of this book, they may arise spontaneously or they may arise through conscious effort, but they don't arise overnight. It takes months, sometimes years, for people to develop the comfort with and understanding of one another that allows them to function with maximum collegial flow (see Chapter 1). Ironically, it takes a great deal of effort to develop the effortless working relationship that characterizes an A Team. But once you have it, it's like lightning in a bottle.

A Teams aren't perfect. (It's the F Troop that believes it can do no wrong.) They make mistakes. But they recover from those mistakes quickly, apologize for anything they've done that has caused problems for others, and learn how to do better next time. An A Team is what Edgar H. Schein, the Sloan Fellows Professor of Management Emeritus at MIT, calls a *learning culture*: It is proactive, dedicated to improvement, eager to communicate relevant information both internally and externally, willing to give others the benefit of the doubt, and committed to understanding challenges in all their diversity and complexity (see Schein, 2010, 366–371).

So, if you try the A Team approach and it doesn't seem to come naturally to people and they make mistakes, don't worry: Just keep at it. The team is just going through some necessary adjustments that will occur during its formation (see Tuckman, 1965). It looks like an A Team is about to be formed at your college or university. Care to try out?

REFERENCES

Buller, J. L., & Reeves, D. M. (2016). *Going for the gold: How to become a world-class academic fundraiser.*

Schein, E. H. (2010). *Organizational culture and leadership.* (4th ed.) San Francisco, CA: Jossey-Bass.

Tuckman, B.W. (1965). Developmental Sequence in Small Groups. *Psychological Bulletin.* 63(6). 384–399.

RESOURCES

Gordon, J. (2013). *The energy bus: 10 rules to fuel your life, work, and team with positive energy.* Hoboken, N.J: Wiley.

Kristof-Brown, A.L., & Billsberry, J. (2013). *Organizational fit: Key issues and new directions.* Chichester, UK: John Wiley and Sons.

Appendix I

What Development Officers (DOs) and Academic Officers (AOs) Need to Know about One Another

If you have a background in development, there are likely to be many aspects of fundraising that you take for granted but that will seem completely new to at least some of the academic administrators you work with. The authors surveyed 665 AOs across the United States and Canada, asking them several questions about how adequately prepared they felt to engage in development activities. Administrators do tend to be involved in fundraising as *contributors*: 84.6% said that they gave cash gifts to their own institutions at least once a year. But they were less commonly involved in securing the contributions of others.

In response to the question "Have you ever engaged in fundraising for a college or university you worked for?," 46.2% replied yes and 53.8% replied no. Those who said that they had indeed engaged in academic fundraising were then asked to specify the largest amount they ever sought from an individual, family, or foundation. (In other words, what was their biggest "ask"?) The answers ranged from $40,000 to five million dollars, with an average of $2.1 million and a median of one million dollars.

When the question then became "What was the largest gift the institution ever received as a result of an ask you made?," the answers ranged from $3,000 to three million dollars, with an average of $510,750 and a median of one million dollars. The fact that the medians kept reverting to a million dollars was predictable. Medians represent the midpoint in a ranked series of numbers, and large asks of a million dollars seem to far outnumber those for any other amount when academic administrators become involved in fundraising. Many deans and department chairs view a million dollars as an almost impossibly large amount of money. But as Number Two (played by Robert Wagner) tells Dr. Evil in Mike Myers' *Austin Powers: International Man of Mystery* (1997), "a million dollars isn't exactly a lot of money these days." One important service that DOs can provide for the academic administrators on their teams is to get them to set their sights on amounts that are realistically attainable in light of donor capacity and institutional need.

When surveyed about their comfort level in asking others for money, they didn't find this task as unpleasant as one might think:

- 46.1% said, "I'm somewhat comfortable doing so."
- 38.4 % said, "I'm very uncomfortable doing so."
- 8.4% said, "I'm neither comfortable nor uncomfortable doing so."
- 7.1% said, "I'm very comfortable doing so."

The administrators were then asked whether the institution where they worked was currently engaged in a capital campaign. A total of 30.8% of the respondents said yes; 69.2% said no. When asked whether their institution was currently planning a capital campaign, 46.1% said yes, 30.6% said no, and 23.3% gave other answers. Among the most common of these other answers were variations of the following:

- My position at my institution isn't one where I would know whether or not a capital campaign is being planned.
- The upper administration is in transition right now, and so no one knows whether a capital campaign is anticipated.
- We always appear to be in the midst of a capital campaign. As soon as one ends, the next one begins.

Academic administrators often feel that the development side of the institution doesn't always understand the goals and needs of academic programs. When asked how well they believed that DOs at their institution truly understood the area in which the academic administrators worked:

- 55.5% said they believed that their areas were somewhat understood by the development staff.
- 24.8% said they believed that the development staff was a bit confused about or misunderstood their areas.
- 19.7% said that they believed the development staff neither understood nor misunderstood their areas.

However, the academic administrators had a bit more confidence in how well they grasped what fundraisers do.

- 53.8% said they believed they understood the work of DOs somewhat.
- 30.7% described themselves as a bit confused or uninformed about the work of DOs.

- 10.3% felt that they neither understood nor misunderstood the work of DOs.
- 5.2% thought that they had an excellent understanding of what DOs do.

Interestingly, none of the respondents described themselves as extremely confused or uninformed about the work of fundraisers.

Nevertheless, when asked what area of development work they wished they had more training in, academic administrators mentioned some fairly basic topics. One cluster of issues (roughly a third of all responses received) dealt with preparing for and completing an ask. Respondents mentioned that they wished their institutions offered them training in how to recognize the right moment to make an ask, how to do so in a way that doesn't make donors feel as though they're being used, how to respond when a prospective donor says no, and even how to hand the solicitation process over to a DO at the proper moment so that the academic administrator isn't the one who actually asks for the money. (It is interesting to contrast how frequently some variant of the last answer came to the claims made in response to the earlier question about whether asking for money was uncomfortable. Roughly half of the people who didn't find asking for money uncomfortable still preferred to have others do it for them.)

About a fifth of the requests for training dealt with how to identify prospective donors or foundations that might provide philanthropic support to their academic areas. The remaining answers were more varied and included such areas as how deans and department chairs can become more actively involved in fundraising if their institutional structures or cultures don't already encourage this activity, how to keep recent alumni sufficiently engaged that they'll support the program throughout their careers, what type of meetings (such as lunches, office calls, invitations, formal gatherings, and the like) prove most effective during the cultivation stage of development, and so on.

If you're a DO who senses that your institution doesn't quite yet have people with the experience and skill to become part of an A Team, it can be worthwhile providing workshops or developing online tutorials on the topics these academic administrators say they need training in most. By learning from the results of our survey of academic administrators, you'll have the information you need as a DO to begin building your A Team from the ground up.

Appendix II

Examples of Certificate/Degree Programs for Development Professionals

While at one time fundraising wasn't a career that one prepared for by means of an academic program, the world of development has become so complex that proper training is quickly becoming a necessity. The following are some of the major academic programs for fundraising professionals that members of any A Team will want to know about. In addition, Seton Hall University maintains a database of university programs that deal with non-profit management (see academic.shu.edu/npo/).

I. *BOARDSOURCE*

BoardSource is a national non-profit organization that provides the highest level of consulting and publications for boards, addressing such issues as the governance, structure, responsibilities, and management of boards. Its mission statement says that "BoardSource is dedicated to advancing the public good by building exceptional nonprofit boards and inspiring board service." (www.boardsource.org/eweb/dynamicpage.aspx?webcode=MissionandPrinc iples) The organization offers a number of training and certificate programs, including

- *The Certificate of Nonprofit Board Education*, designed for new and potential board members as well as staff members and consultants who are new to working with a board.
- *The Leadership Certificate for Nonprofit Board Chairs*, intended for board chairs who are looking for practical approaches to some of the most challenging aspects of the job.

- *The Leadership Certificate for Nonprofit Chief Executives*, focuses on the needs of chief executives who are committed to building a constructive partnership with their board.

BoardSource also has a very active training schedule, including seminars at various locations, webinars, an annual conference, and digital instruction opportunities. For more information, contact

BoardSource
750 9th Street NW, Suite 650
Washington, DC 20001
202-349-2500
www.boardsource.org

II. *THE ASSOCIATION OF FUNDRAISING PROFESSIONALS* (AFP)

The mission statement of the AFP states that "AFP, an association of professionals throughout the world, advances philanthropy by enabling people and organizations to practice ethical and effective fundraising. AFP offers education, training, mentoring, research, credentialing and advocacy" (www.afpnet.org/About/content.cfm?ItemNumber=4385). As a way of fulfilling the last goal of this mission statement, AFP offers several different programs for professional development along with an annual calendar of conferences and training programs. Its regular programs include

The Certified Fund Raising Executive (CFRE) Program

The CFRE credential provides objective documentation of personal and professional achievement and commitment.

The Advanced Certified Fundraising Executive (ACFRE) Program

The ACFRE credential signifies an advanced mastery of professional standards in leadership, management and ethics.

The Professional Development in Fundraising Diploma—Spanish Language

This highly innovative program is a partnership between AFP and Tecnológico de Monterrey that results in an online diploma certifying that the student has attained a certain level of competence in a range of fundraising issues, particularly those that are important Latin America. Tecnológico de Monterrey, based in Monterrey, Mexico, is a multi-campus university system with academic centers in different regions of Mexico and an extensive online virtual university. Its Social Leaders program, of which this online diploma is a part, has a long history of serving students by preparing them to meet the needs of a rapidly changing world.

III. *THE COUNCIL FOR THE ADVANCEMENT AND SUPPORT OF EDUCATION (CASE)*

CASE is a professional international association serving educational institutions and the advancement professionals who work on their behalf. CASE offers numerous programs throughout the year, from institutes that focus on specific topics in fundraising to an annual summit, which is designed for the senior level of professionals in higher education advancement. CASE programs are useful meetings for an entire A Team to attend since they focus on the needs, not just of development officers (DOs), but also of faculty members and academic administrators who are involved in fundraising activities.

IV. *MAJOR CREDIT-BEARING PROGRAMS*

A. The *George H. Heyman, Jr., Center for Philanthropy and Fundraising*, part of New York University's School of Professional Studies, offers a master's of science degree in fundraising and grant making, as well as additional non-credit certificate programs, courses, workshops, and webinars. The program states that

> Through in-depth analyses of the legal, financial, ethical, psychological, and historical aspects of philanthropy, students learn to implement successful outreach practices—including direct mail, telecommunications, social media, and special events—and to gain a comprehensive understanding of giving and grant evaluation within non-profit organizations. In addition, they explore the impact of globalization on philanthropy, the development of boards, and the economic and statistical underpinnings of fundraising reporting (http://www.scps.nyu.edu/about/newsroom/news/2014/nyu_school_of_contin_1.html).

B. The *Lilly Family School of Philanthropy at Indiana University* offers degrees in philanthropic studies at all levels: bachelor's, master's, and doctorate: The school seeks to increase "the understanding of philanthropy and [to improve] its practice worldwide through critical inquiry, interdisciplinary research, teaching, training, and civic engagement" (www.philanthropy.iupui.edu/the-schools-mission). Programs are offered in various areas through different schools and institutes:

- *The Fund Raising School* "teaches comprehensive, proven fundraising concepts and principles, incorporating the latest research. At the same time, it offers specific tools and techniques that enable and empower fundraisers to effectively plan and manage developmental efforts" (www.philanthropy.iupui.edu/the-fund-raising-school-courses).
- *The Lake Institute on Faith and Giving* "exists to explore the relationship between faith and giving in various religious traditions. ... Studying, teaching and understanding the religious motivations for giving allows for more effective fundraising and outreach across the nonprofit sector" (www.philanthropy.iupui.edu/lake-about-us).
- *The Women's Philanthropy Institute* "studies how and why gender matters in philanthropy. Men's and women's motivations for giving and patterns of giving differ. What works for men in philanthropy may not work for women. ... [The program is intended to] provide key insights into women's philanthropy and women's giving, allowing your organization to be successful in engaging women as donors" (www.philanthropy. iupui.edu/womens-philanthropy-institute-courses).

C. *The Stanford Center on Philanthropy and Civil Society* (PACS) "develops and shares knowledge to improve philanthropy, strengthen civil society and effect social change" (pacscenter.stanford.edu/overview). PACS offers individual courses, PhD and Post-Doctoral Fellowships, conferences and other types of training programs in addition to its degree programs.

D. *Northeastern University* offers a graduate certificate in Nonprofit Sector, Philanthropy, and Social Change. The program notes that this certificate was developed "as a response to recent developments in social change theory," practice, and funding that are placing new demands and expectations on social change actors in the non-profit, public, and private sectors, including non-profit leaders, philanthropists, policy makers, and corporate social responsibility managers. These developments include the emergence of hybrid, cross-sector business models and new intermediary mechanisms for channeling the flow of capital into social change; new expectations and standards for performance measurement, transparency, and accountability; more sophisticated use of data and technology to support decision making, evaluation, and continual improvement; decreased public funding for traditional non-profit activities; and "the emergence of social media as a vehicle for mobilizing people and resources" (www.northeastern. edu/cssh/policyschool/graduate-programs/graduate-certificate-nonprofit-sector-philanthropy-social-change/).

To earn the certificate, students take two required courses (Nonprofit Organizations and Social Change and The Nonprofit Sector in Civil Society and Public Affairs) in a curriculum that is professionally oriented and application-based. It is anticipated that most students in the program will be seeking leadership positions in non-profit organizations or in a public agency that deals extensively with non-profits.

E. *St. Mary's University of Minnesota* offers a master's of arts degree in Philanthropy & Development that takes place over a two-year period and incorporates three ten-day summer residencies. The coursework involves classes in leadership and critical thinking as well as such areas of development as board governance, ethics in fundraising, and major giving.

F. *The University of Northern Iowa* offers a master's of arts degree in Philanthropy and Nonprofit Development that may be completed entirely online. "The primary goal of this program is to develop and enhance professional skills and knowledge in philanthropy (e.g., cause marketing, strategic planning) and the non-profit sectors. A unique feature of this master's degree is that the course sequence allows students to complete their research papers while simultaneously completing course assignments" (www.uni.edu/continuinged/distance/philanthropy/faq#t16n978)

G. *Bay Path University* in Longmeadow, Massachusetts, offers numerous graduate degrees related to advancement. Its master's of science degree in Nonprofit Management and Philanthropy consists of twelve three-credit courses, each taught in an accelerated format over eight weeks. Its master's of science degree in Strategic Fundraising and Philanthropy has two tracks: one in non-profit fundraising and the other in higher education fundraising. All programs are available in online versions.

Appendix III

Certified Fund Raising Executive (CFRE) Examination Content Outline

The following is an outline of the areas covered on the exam to become a CFRE. It is presented here both to encourage current development officers (DOs) to seek CFRE certification and because it provides an excellent summary of what today's DO is expected to know. As members of an A Team continue to work together to improve their knowledge and skills, the topics covered by the CFRE exam provide an excellent source of ideas for discussions, workshops, retreats, and other training opportunities.

Reprinted with permission from www.cfre.org/wp-content/uploads/2013/08/Test-Content-Outline-06.01.13.pdf. Modified only to adapt British to American spelling.

CURRENT AND PROSPECTIVE DONOR RESEARCH 16%—28 ITEMS

A. Develop a list of prospective donors by identifying individuals and groups (foundations, corporations, government agencies, etc.) who have the capacity and propensity to give, in order to qualify prospective donors for further research and cultivation efforts.
B. Implement and utilize a secure data management system that stores information about current and prospective donors to enable segmented retrieval and analysis.
C. Analyze the list of current and prospective donors using characteristics such as demographics, interests, values, giving history, relationships, and linkages to the organization, in order to select potential donors for particular projects and fundraising programs.

D. Rate current and prospective donors in categories of giving potential in order to prioritize and plan cultivation and solicitation.

E. Present the list of current and prospective donors and relevant information to organizational leaders in order to establish consensus for action.

KEY KNOWLEDGE AREAS FOR THE ABOVE TASKS

- Indicators that identify trends and define characteristics (such as socioeconomic, giving history, generational, gender and cultural) of a constituency.
- Donor acquisition strategies.
- Sources of financial support (such as individuals, corporations, grant-making bodies, foundations, government).
- Types of information needed to identify prospective donors and determine specific fundraising strategies.
- Donor profile components.
- Indicators of gift potential.
- Donor giving patterns.
- Data analysis techniques (such as statistical analysis, data mining, and segmentation).
- Data gathering techniques (such as surveys, focus groups, interviews, social networking).
- Elements of a comprehensive data management system (including data capture, storage, retrieval, maintenance, and security).
- Prospect screening, qualifying, and rating methods.
- Motivations, practices, and policies of various funding sources.
- Prospect information sources (such as people, written/published, and electronic/online) and their uses and limitations.
- Elements of components of a fundraising program, including annual, capital/major, and planned giving/legacies.
- Relationships between and among annual, capital/major, and planned giving/legacies programs.
- Donor survey components and uses.
- Market study components and uses.
- Privacy legislation and the ethical use of data.

SECURING THE GIFT 19%—34 ITEMS

A. Develop a compelling case for support by involving stakeholders (such as volunteers, staff, and members of the Board) in order to communicate the rationale for supporting the organization's fundraising program.

B. Apply prospect research data to develop a solicitation plan for involvement of individual donors and/or donor groups.
C. Plan a comprehensive solicitation program in order to generate financial support for the organization's purpose.
D. Prepare donor-focused and segmented solicitation communications in order to influence and facilitate informed gift decisions.
E. Ask for and secure gifts from prospects in order to generate financial support for the organization's purpose.
F. Evaluate the solicitation program using appropriate criteria and methodology in order to produce accurate analytic reports for effective decision making.

KEY KNOWLEDGE AREAS FOR THE ABOVE TASKS

- Psychology of giving.
- Sociological and cultural influences on giving.
- Elements and uses of a case statement and a case for support.
- Types of gifts (cash, securities, property, gifts in kind, etc.).
- Solicitation strategies and their effectiveness with different donor groups.
- Fundraising techniques and programs such as
  - Direct marketing (mail, telephone, electronic, direct response television (DRTV), etc.).
  - Special events (dinners, walk-a-thons, tournaments, auctions, etc.).
  - Grant proposal writing (foundations, corporations, government, etc.).
  - Corporate sponsorships, partnerships, and cause-related marketing.
  - Gift planning (such as bequests, legacies, trusts).
  - Major gifts.
  - Memorial and tribute gifts.
  - Capital and endowment campaigns.
  - Membership and alumni programs.
  - Gaming and lottery programs.
  - Workforce and payroll giving/federated campaigns.
  - Street collections/face-to-face solicitation.
  - For-profit activities (such as product sales and charity/thrift shops).
  - Community and third-party fundraising.
- Other
  - Feasibility study components and uses.
  - Negotiation techniques.
  - External factors that may affect the viability of the organization and its programs/services.
  - Tangible and intangible ways in which donors benefit from giving.

- Peer-to-peer principles and their application to fundraising.
- Fundraising program evaluation standards, procedures, and methods (including benchmark calculations such as cost of fundraising, Return On Investment (ROI), fundraising ratios, average gift, response rates).
- Payment structures for contributions (outright, pledge, installment, etc.).
- Communication methods and messages to reach target audiences.
- The use of prospect research to inform cultivation and solicitation strategies.
- Involvement of donor advisors.
- Use of electronic media in solicitation (email, text messaging, widgets, etc.).

RELATIONSHIP BUILDING 27%—48 ITEMS

A. Initiate and strengthen relationships with all constituents through a systematic cultivation plan designed to build trust in, and long term commitment to, the organization.
B. Develop and implement a comprehensive communications plan in order to inform constituents and identified markets about the mission, vision, and values of the organization, its funding priorities, and gift opportunities.
C. Promote a culture of philanthropy by broadening constituents' understanding of the value of giving.
D. Acknowledge and recognize gifts in ways that are meaningful to donors and appropriate to the mission and values of the organization.

KEY KNOWLEDGE AREAS FOR THE ABOVE TASKS

- Elements of a cultivation plan.
- Components of a comprehensive communications plan and processes for creating one.
- Donor acquisition and retention principles.
- Communication methods and messages to reach target audiences.
- Oral and written communication techniques.
- Components and uses of active listening.
- Aspects of nonverbal communication (body language, eye contact, etc.).
- Interpersonal communication (e.g., trust building, team building, group dynamics).
- External spheres of influence (such as corporate, governmental, social, civic, professional, and religious leadership) and their interrelationships.
- Methods for optimizing relationships between and among constituencies.
- Relationship between philanthropy and fundraising.
- Benefits of fundraising programs for organizations.

- Relationship strengthening using incentives (such as member benefits, special invitations, premiums, naming rights).
- Donor recognition techniques.
- Use of electronic media in relationship building (social networking, video sharing, etc.).

VOLUNTEER INVOLVEMENT 8%—14 ITEMS

A. Create a structured process for the identification, recruitment, evaluation, recognition, and replacement of volunteers, in order to strengthen the organization's effectiveness.
B. Empower and support volunteers by providing orientation, training, and specific job descriptions in order to enhance the volunteers' effectiveness.
C. Engage volunteers in the fundraising process and related activities in order to expand organizational capacity.
D. Participate in recruiting experienced and diverse leadership on boards and/ or committees in order to ensure that these groups are representative of, and responsive to, the communities served.

KEY KNOWLEDGE AREAS FOR THE ABOVE TASKS

- Personality types and attributes.
- Volunteer roles in fundraising.
- Volunteer job description components and uses.
- Principles of adult learning.
- Skills training and competency development methods.
- Strategies for optimizing volunteers' time and talent.
- Volunteer recruitment, management, motivation, retention, recognition, and evaluation techniques.
- Governance principles and models for not-for-profit organizations.
- Value of diversity and community representation.
- Respective roles of volunteer board members and staff with respect to governance and management.

LEADERSHIP AND MANAGEMENT 18%—32 ITEMS

A. Foster and support a culture of philanthropy across the organization and its constituencies.
B. Ensure sound administrative and management policies and procedures to support fundraising functions.

C. Participate in the organization's strategic planning process in order to ensure the integration of fundraising and philanthropy.
D. Design and implement short- and long-term fundraising plans and budgets in order to support the organization's strategic goals.
E. Apply key principles of marketing and public relations to fundraising planning and programs.
F. Conduct ongoing performance analysis of the fundraising program using accepted and appropriate standards in order to identify opportunities, resolve problems, and inform future planning.
G. Recruit, train, and support staff by applying human resource principles in order to foster professionalism and a productive team-oriented work environment.
H. Contract for services in order to optimize the efforts of the fundraising function.

KEY KNOWLEDGE AREAS FOR THE ABOVE TASKS

- Components and uses of mission and vision statements.
- Strategic and action planning methods.
- Fundraising program evaluation standards, procedures, and methods (including benchmark calculations such as cost of fundraising, ROI, fundraising ratios, average gift, response rates).
- Policy development procedures.
- Elements of a fundraising plan.
- Place of fundraising in the strategic planning process.
- Impact of organizational structures and team dynamics on the effectiveness of fundraising programs.
- Methods for ensuring the integrity of data management and record-keeping systems.
- Components and uses of development audits.
- Financial management, including budgeting and financial statements.
- Use and application of market research.
- Marketing and public relations principles.
- Benefits of a media program.
- Methods for assessing the organization's impact on the community.
- Training resources appropriate to the different fundraising program elements.
- Staff recruitment, managing, retaining, rewarding, and evaluating techniques.
- Culture and definition of philanthropy.
- Tools to assess the need for contracted services (e.g., gap analysis).

- Techniques for selecting, evaluating, and managing contracted services.
- Principles of managing meetings.
- Methods and strategies for managing change.
- Principles of effective leadership.
- Sources of historical and contemporary information about philanthropy and fundraising.

ETHICS AND ACCOUNTABILITY 11%—19 ITEMS

A. Ensure that all fundraising activities are conducted in accordance with ethical principles and standards.
B. Create gift acceptance policies that reflect the values of the organization and satisfy legal and ethical standards.
C. Clarify, implement, monitor, and honor donors' intent and instructions, and ensure that allocations are accurately documented in the organization's records.
D. Report to constituents the sources, uses, impact, and management of donated funds in order to preserve and enhance confidence and public trust in the organization.
E. Comply with all reporting requirements and regulations in order to fulfill commitment to accountability and demonstrate transparency.

KEY KNOWLEDGE AREAS FOR THE ABOVE TASKS

- Laws and regulations affecting not-for-profit organizations, including interactions with their stakeholders (donors, staff, volunteers, etc.).
- Legal and ethical practices related to donor record maintenance, gift accounting, and audit trails.
- Methods of recording, receipting, recognizing, and acknowledging gifts.
- Elements of gift acceptance policies.
- Elements of gift agreements.
- Accounting principles for not-for-profit organizations.
- Organizational transparency, including methods for reporting fundraising performance, outcomes, and impact to constituencies.
- Donor Bill of Rights/Donors' Charter.
- Personal privacy and information protection.
- Ethical principles relevant to cultivation, securing and accepting gifts.
- Methods and processes for ethical decision making.

Appendix IV

Training at Your Institution

ATLAS: Academic Training, Leadership, & Assessment Services offers training programs, books, and materials that deal with many aspects of academic leadership, collegiality, and fundraising. Its programs include the following:

- Decision Making
- Problem Solving
- Work-Life Balance
- Time Management
- Stress Management
- Conflict Management
- Promoting Teamwork
- Promoting Collegiality
- Communicating Effectively
- Leading Meetings Effectively
- Managing Projects Effectively
- Positive Academic Leadership
- Best Practices in Faculty Evaluation
- Creating a Culture of Student Success
- Change Leadership in Higher Education
- The Fundamentals of Academic Leadership
- Going for the Gold: How to Become a World-Class Academic Fundraiser
- World-Class Fundraising Isn't a Spectator Sport: The Team Approach to Academic Fundraising

These programs are offered in half-day, full-day, and multi-day formats. ATLAS also offers reduced prices on leadership books, the Collegiality Assessment Matrix (CAM) and Self-Assessment Matrix (S-AM), which allow academic programs to evaluate the collegiality and civility of their faculty members in a consistent, objective, and reliable manner, and other instruments to assess faculty and staff engagement or morale. The monthly ATLAS E-Newsletter addresses a variety of issues related to academic leadership and is sent free to subscribers.

For more information, contact

ATLAS: Academic Training, Leadership, & Assessment Services
4521 PGA Boulevard, PMB 186
Palm Beach Gardens, FL 33418
800-355-6742; www.atlasleadership.com
Email: questions@atlasleadership.com

About the Authors

JEFFREY L. BULLER has served in administrative positions ranging from department chair to VP for academic affairs at four very different institutions: Loras College, Georgia Southern University, Mary Baldwin College, and Florida Atlantic University. He is the author of thirteen books on higher education administration, a textbook for first year college students, and a book of essays on the music dramas of Richard Wagner. Dr. Buller has also written numerous articles on Greek and Latin literature, nineteenth- and twentieth-century opera, and college administration. From 2003 to 2005, he served as the principal English-language lecturer at the International Wagner Festival in Bayreuth, Germany.

More recently, he has been active as a consultant to the Ministry of Education in Saudi Arabia, where he is assisting with the creation of a kingdom-wide Academic Leadership Center. Along with Robert E. Cipriano, Dr. Buller is a senior partner in ATLAS: Academic Training, Leadership, & Assessment Services, through which he has presented numerous workshops on academic leadership and fundraising.

DIANNE M. REEVES has enjoyed success in three distinct industries and has held leadership positions spanning more than thirty-five years in nursing, small business management/program development, and higher education advancement. She began her development work at the university level as an advisor to legendary football head coach Howard Schnellenberger. Experienced in marketing and development, Ms. Reeves has also worked as a non-profit consultant and financial systems manager. She has served as a board member for the Palm Beach County chapter of the Association of Fundraising Professionals and the Planned Giving Council of Palm Beach County and as a member of Executive Women of Palm Beach. Ms. Reeves believes that each sector of her work experience has molded her philanthropic approach to the whole person by giving her a more complete understanding of psychology, business, and non-profit priorities. To date in her development work, she has raised well over $45 million for Florida Atlantic University. In this capacity, she sees herself as making a major contribution to the mission and vision of that institution.

In addition to a master's degree in business administration, Ms. Reeves has earned several professional certifications in fundraising, most notably the Certified Fund Raising Executive (CFRE), Chartered Advisory in Philanthropy, and Certified Governance Trainer and remains involved with numerous professional organizations. While she has authored numerous articles in nursing, this book and its companion volume are her first publications in the realm of advancement.